WISE THOUGHTS FOR DOERS

A Walk In Inspiration and Testimony

Nathan W. Palus

WestBow Press books may be ordered through booksellers or by contacting:

WestBow Press
A Division of Thomas Nelson & Zondervan
1663 Liberty Drive
Bloomington, IN 47403
www.westbowpress.com
1 (866) 928-1240

ISBN: 978-1-5127-2913-9 (sc)
ISBN: 978-1-5127-2914-6 (hc)
ISBN: 978-1-5127-2912-2 (e)

Library of Congress Control Number: 2016901727

Print information available on the last page.

WestBow Press rev. date: 02/08/2016

Contents

“The fear of the Lord is the beginning of knowledge, but fools despise wisdom and discipline” (Proverbs 1:7).

If we are asked questions about life at age five or ten, our answers will be much different than if we are asked those same questions at age twenty or twenty-five.

As we gain insight into living, those questions should elicit answers of far greater clarity, depth, and complexity at age forty or forty-five.

That has been my experience, and the things I have learned helped provide the foundation for this book.

Children of One God

Even in this age of uncertainty, all of us human beings can be sure we were born of a woman. Granted, with today's scientific and technological advances, some of us might have started in a test tube or a petri dish before being placed inside the womb. But the fact remains that the womb is the place best suited to nurture and to grow a fetus and to bring it to birth.

Darwin claimed humans evolved from apes, but in Genesis, the first book of the Bible, God tells the story of how He created the human species. Man was created from the dust, and God breathed life into him. He then gave that first man, Adam, a companion or helper by placing him into a deep sleep and taking a rib from him to create Eve. This He did through His glory and majesty (Genesis 2).

The world is deeply divided over whether there is one sovereign God, many gods, or any God at all. With humanity splintered into many factions—including adherents of monotheism, polytheism, pantheism—there is a wide variety of religions and forms of worship. Atheists, of course, refuse to worship.

Religion and worship have spawned epic disagreements, splitting groups and societies throughout the world. The same questions have always plagued humanity. Who or what should be worshiped? And what methods of worship are the right ones?

Solomon rightly says, "The fear of the Lord is the beginning of knowledge, but fools despise wisdom and discipline" (Proverbs 1:7). However, we have failed to see the truth of this.

Religion and worship have become the matches that have ignited tinderboxes around the world. The resulting strife has continually marginalized God and has prevented the recognition of His truth. In many places, people have replaced God's supremacy with those powerless things that God Himself has made. Many societies have created anthropocentric systems with little discipline or wisdom. Some men and women of the cloth have established themselves as demigods and potentates, sitting in high positions over congregations large and small; they pontificate, polarize, and sometimes even poison the weak, who rely on them to show the way to obtain faith or regain it.

Jesus Christ, the Son of God, has been moved out of the way. He has been placed on the sidelines as these prideful buffoons seek accolades and worship, never forgetting to hit up their followers for money. They can bring in donations at church services or online, with cash and credit cards eagerly accepted. Preaching the gospel is a lucrative venture for some. Although they may preach Jesus Christ as Lord, their prideful behavior makes them lords over their congregants.

The weak, who are already at a disadvantage, are lured into accepting these people as powerful men and women who can heal and bless them. Often no one mentions that Jesus Christ is the source of their power. The Lord can and does make miracles happen, and He can heal people by using flawed human beings. We must realize that these humans are only channels for such miracles. They are just as flawed as anyone else; we are all sinners and have come short of the glory of God (Romans 3:23).

I would be remiss if I did not mention the sexual sinfulness in ministry. To some, sex is a natural benefit that comes with a position of power and leadership. Some who are being led derive satisfaction from being selected as the sexual partners of the rich and the powerful. Leaders will often fill the innocent and the unlearned with fear and shame to keep them bound and submissive.

Money and gifts are of no consequence to some givers, because these things do not come from their own earnings or accounts. In some ministries, finances are secrets closely guarded by the leaders or by a select few. This makes it easy to continue in sin. Certainly, it is not a bad thing to have the head of a ministry involved in making decisions about church funds; however, even those proclaiming the gospel are not immune to dishonesty.

So the key is to keep a level head and to make sure God resides in a leader. A good shepherd takes good care of the sheep and is a servant. The other key is to know the Word, because the Word is life. "In the beginning was the Word, and the Word was with God, and the Word was God" (John 1:1). It is incumbent on all of us to know God.

We know that the Word became flesh and dwelt among us. The Word is Jesus Christ, who was born of a woman—Mary, a virgin girl—and who was perfect and without sin. Yet He bore our sins so that we could be redeemed from them.

Paul implores us to "do your best to present yourself to God as one approved, a workman who does not need to be ashamed and who correctly handles the word of truth. Avoid godless chatter because those who indulge in it will become more and more ungodly" (2 Timothy 2:15–16). Paul also emphasizes that "bad teaching will spread like gangrene" (2 Timothy 2:17).

Gangrene is a deadly infection that will spread once it takes hold of the body. It can kill you if it is not readily diagnosed and quickly treated. Gangrene is caused when dead cells are infected by bacteria due to a lack of blood flow. Methods of eradication must be precise; debridement and amputation of limbs are sometimes necessary to save lives.

The lifestyles of those who preach the Word of God and present themselves as models must meet with God's approval, and therefore they should not infect or lead others to spiritual death by misleading them.

If we are searching for the truth and wish to serve the Lord in His beauty and holiness, we must take to heart Paul's edifying words: "Nevertheless, God's solid foundation stands firm, sealed with this inscription: 'The Lord knows those who are his,' and 'Everyone who confesses the name of the Lord must turn away from wickedness'" (2 Timothy 2:19).

We who are Christians serving the true God in Jesus must recognize what has infected us and is stopping the redemptive flow of Christ's blood within us. We ought to seek our cure in the only one who can cut away what is foreign and sinful in us. All human beings must seek Jesus. He is readily available. "Seek the Lord while he may be found; call on him while he is near. Let the wicked forsake his ways and the evil man his thoughts, let him turn to the Lord, and he will have mercy on him, and to our God, for he will freely pardon" (Isaiah 55:6–7).

The Lord judges the non-Christian, but He also offers salvation. If anyone committing sin repents in earnest, the Lord, who sees the heart, will respond. The prophet Isaiah relayed the Lord's words to his rebellious people, and those words still apply to anyone who goes astray. He said, "I revealed myself to those who did not ask for me; I was found by those who did not seek me. To a nation that did not call on my name, I said, 'Here am I, here am I'" (Isaiah 65:1).

So what do we say to our detractors, who continually deter others from finding or living the truth? What do we say when they rant and rave about how our God is a bloody and angry God? We can respond in truth, for God told Isaiah to remind His people of this: "All day long I have held out my hands to an obstinate people, who walk in ways not good, pursuing their own imaginations" (Isaiah 65:2). If those who disobeyed had taken His hand, He would not have had to shed their blood or to cast them into the pit.

It is not wrong to exercise our imaginations. However, if we have no foundation in God, we may find ourselves wondering off into oblivion without a compass to guide us back to the lighthouse of faith. Our imaginations should serve us. We ought not to serve our imaginations. We must not go beyond boundaries and into restricted areas that may not be safe. When we allow ourselves to become slaves to our imaginations, our spirits and our bodies become entrapped. Imagination manifests into actions, and unchecked actions become disasters.

Picture a hot-air balloon that is completely fueled and untethered, with the elements deciding where it goes, how long it stays afloat, and whether it lands or crashes. This is not a good scenario considering all that could go wrong.

God waits for all of His children. Because of His love for us, He sent his only Son to die for us on a cross at Calvary that we might have eternal life. Jesus Christ awaits our knock on that door to salvation. He will swing the door wide open to receive us. Consider John 3:16.

New Year's Resolutions vs. Resolutions of Faith

Toward the end of each year, many of us consider how we can change our lives. We make New Year's resolutions and at the start of the year vigorously attempt to follow the path chosen to reach our goals. All too often, we fail and give up even before the first month has passed. A New Year's resolution is very different from a resolution of faith. Attempting to discern these marked differences is a good thing. Discernment is a gift from God, and the ability to make a resolution of faith is a blessing. Doing this is a way to know God and His Word.

The New King James Version of the Bible aptly describes faith as something present and affirmative: "Now faith is the substance of things hoped for, the evidence of things not seen" (Hebrews 11:1). The New International Version offers a simpler description: "Now faith is being sure of what we hope for and certain of what we do not see." Both translations show the benefits of knowing the Word, which is the road map to our desired result.

What force drives us toward our goals? Can we discern that force? We have always heard that a positive force is better than a negative force since the wind drives our sails, and that is certainly true when it comes to making resolutions of faith. We can be sure of accomplishing our goals if we have faith in Jesus Christ and cultivate a relationship with Him.

Jesus Christ lived, died, and was resurrected from the dead, and though we were not present at these events, we still believe that they took place and that His sacrifice transcends our lives today. We are certain of what we did not see with the naked eye and certain of the things to come that we see in the Spirit.

Armed with this knowledge, we who are resolute in faith are being pushed forward and compelled by the Spirit of God in Jesus Christ, who is capable of moving every barrier we face. We often think that the only way to move a barrier is to pick it up and to toss it aside. But wisdom tells us that to believe this is the only solution is false and limiting. For example, we could climb over, jump over, go under, or walk around a barrier to get to our destination without lifting something that might be many times our weight and then trying to heave it out of our path.

Let us look in the Scriptures for instances of committed believing that brought remarkable results. In Exodus 3, we read that Moses approached the mountain of God, and on that mountain he saw a burning bush. After this had caught his curiosity, an angel of God appeared to him, and so he said to himself, *The bush is burning but is not being consumed. I will go up and investigate this phenomenon.* When Moses drew closer, the Lord God called out to him from inside the burning bush, "Moses! Moses!" (Exodus 3:4).

Moses answered, "Here I am." God then began a conversation with him, first establishing His holiness by telling Moses, "Do not come any closer. Take off your sandals, for the place where you are standing is holy ground" (Exodus 3:5). God explained their connection through a deified lineage of father to children, patriarch to patriots, and a God who hurts when His children hurt. He told Moses,

> I am the God of your father, the God of Abraham, the God of Isaac and the God of Jacob. I

> have indeed seen the misery of my people in Egypt. I have heard them crying out because of their slave drivers, and I am concerned about their suffering. So I have come down to rescue them from the hands of the Egyptians and to bring them up out of that land into a good and spacious land, a land flowing with milk and honey – the home of the Canaanites, Hittites, Amorites, Perizzites, Hivites, and Jebusites. And now the cry of the Israelites has reached me, and I have seen the way the Egyptians are oppressing them. So now, go. I am sending you to Pharaoh to bring my people the Israelites out of Egypt. (Exodus 3:5–10)

God explained to Moses who He was and what His connection was to Moses and to the children of Israel enslaved in Egypt, assigning Moses the job of freeing the Israelites. If the Lord God demonstrated the truth as vividly and dramatically to you as He did to Moses, would you doubt anything He said to you or about you? If He gave you a task to do, would you believe that He knew you could do the task? His directives always come with the omnipotence He possesses. By his power He awakens innate abilities to complete any task He assigns. Do you believe in His power to transcend all and to bring about transformation in anyone?

You should believe that the Lord will make you fit for an assigned task, but as we venture further into Exodus we will see that if you do not believe this, you are not alone. Moses had the same misgivings. He was not convinced. Moses allowed his experiences, especially the last one he had in Egypt before fleeing into the desert, to sabotage his confidence. Moses had killed a man, an Egyptian task master who had been abusing a Hebrew slave. In that instant, Moses, recognizing that he too was a Hebrew, became an enemy of Egypt and its pharaoh. The abuse of the Hebrew people had affected his heart and his spirit. He had to do something to stop the abuse he saw, and that step was physical.

Moses felt terror upon hearing that Pharaoh sought to kill him. Fear in some situations freezes mind and body, but Moses was not paralyzed. He fled into the desert and reached as far as Midian where he took up new residence. For countless individuals though, fear can bring inaction, preventing success and stifling breakthroughs.

Still, Moses questioned his ability to carry out this task, asking God, "Who am I, that I should go to Pharaoh and bring the Israelites out of Egypt?" (Exodus 3:11). Certainly Moses remembered the circumstances by which he ended up traversing the desert and becoming a husband, father, and shepherd in the household of his father-in-law Jethro. Moses had begun a new life. He needed convincing that he could return to Egypt and face the people who were enslaving his fellow Hebrews, the people for whom he had previously killed and the people he was being sent to deliver.

Have you ever felt that the person or situation that you should embrace wholeheartedly would oppose you? It is common to feel like that at the beginning, or maybe most of the way, or even all of the way! Moses remembered seeing two Hebrew men fighting each other the day after he had killed the Egyptian. When he scolded the one in the wrong, the man responded, "Who made you ruler and judge over us? Are you thinking of killing me as you killed the Egyptian?" (Exodus 2:14).

In that instant, fear had introduced itself, telling Moses, "I am going to visit with you for a while." Moses had been saddled with that encounter and still felt its weight as he stood before God at the burning bush. Fear is a frontal attack on God's will and purpose through His people, but God cannot be cowed. Fear has no place in Him, and so it must be uprooted and destroyed from within the human spirit. "For God did not give us a spirit of timidity, but a spirit of power, of love and of self-discipline" (2 Timothy 1:7).

Surmounting fear is not an easy task. We must first learn the truth, and in learning the truth, we will be unlearning and displacing what occupies our minds and masquerades as the truth. Moses had just begun to learn about himself and where he belonged in God's plan. He was born a Hebrew, though he had been raised as an Egyptian in the house of Pharaoh. He needed to be taught many things to replace the fear and the uncertainty within him.

Sometimes it takes years of teaching, coaching, and cajoling before we can conquer our fears and move forward boldly. God had to teach Moses many things by answering his questions and by telling him how to handle situations before he was satisfied that he could perform his task in Egypt.

God reassured Moses that He would be with him every step of the way while he was in Egypt. God promised that after Moses had accomplished the task set before him, He would allow Moses and all the children of Israel to return to the same mountain, the place of the burning bush, to worship Him. This would prove that He was God and that He was with them.

But at the time, Moses thought, *That's easy for You to say, God, but You don't understand these people. Look what I did to protect that Hebrew, the one I killed for, and then look at how the others saw my action and how they treated me for intervening on their behalf.*

The "What If" Question

What if I say, and what if I do? What if they don't believe me or even in you? The "what ifs" are usually much stronger than we know, and they fuel the fears that defeat us in our quest for freedom, success, love, spiritual fulfillment, wisdom, and everything else that matters in our lives. They can elicit responses much like that of the Peanuts character who says, "Good grief, Charlie Brown." He is, in effect, telling Charlie, "Can we just get on with it? Why are you making such a big deal out of something so small?" The person who cannot discern the root of the problem cannot help us fix it.

Our Lord God is a discerner of all things, and He offered Moses solutions to his concerns and fears every time the prophet posed a question. He has answers and plans for all of us. We will recognize this when we learn to put God first in all that we attempt to do. If our actions are not godly ones, He will not support us in those endeavors, but knowledge of God helps us to discern the right choices, leading us to great achievements. The book of Exodus chronicles the great achievements of Moses as he allowed the power of almighty God to lead him, and I encourage you to read Exodus and the rest of the Bible.

Proverbs 10:8 says, "The wise in heart accept commands, but a chattering fool comes to ruin."

As we examine the art of making and keeping commitments through resolutions of faith, let us first look at the factor of youth versus adulthood and maturation. The proverb says, "The wise in heart accept commands," but the heart alone won't bring us to such a place. The brain plays a great role in guiding the heart, because without a functional brain, we couldn't grasp even the most minuscule ideas, let alone manage the complex calculations needed to make wise decisions. The necessary brainpower is available from childhood through all the stages of maturation.

The second part of the proverb also holds true at all stages: "a chattering fool comes to ruin." At any age, we must have the discipline to shut out chaos, because without this discipline we invite failure. Great communication skills and great social skills coupled with knowledge of God will help us to keep resolutions of faith.

Putting these three components together will bring about an epiphany like the one Paul describes: "When I was a child, I talked like a child, I thought like a child, I reasoned like a child. When I became a man, I put childish ways behind me" (1 Corinthians 13:11). It took Paul some time to develop into the great apostle he became. Paul was well educated, but that education had blinded him. He zealously persecuted Christians until the day he met Jesus Christ on the road to Damascus. Only then did he become a true man.

We can possess perfect physical features, but mentally and spiritually we can be desperately deficient as human beings. Our life experiences sculpt us as persons as do the cultures in which we are reared. We must not hang on to counterproductive attitudes. The Peanuts character Linus can't imagine being without his security blanket. That blanket is just a piece of cloth and has no redeeming powers or anointing by the Holy Spirit.

Attitudes are learned behaviors and can be unlearned if we open ourselves to reason. The alternative is that we can continue in a childlike state, clinging to our security blankets and refusing to strengthen our social and faith skills, thus retarding our growth.

Our attitudes can and will change because of a lifelong socialization process. This begins with our parents and our families and continues through organizations or affiliations such as schools, churches, clubs, professions, and nations. The question is whether we will allow change to take root or whether we will try to rebuff change.

Parental influences weaken as a child grows older and encounters new social influences that quite often require a consistent commitment. Such consistency in thought and action is necessary to preserve harmony among people with varying belief systems, feelings, and behavioral patterns. This effort shapes our attitudes. The person who resists creates dissonance in the group.

Dissonance is not always bad, because sometimes we need a revelation of the truth, new information that will cause us to change our minds about something.

New facts can easily change our attitudes. They can cause us to disagree and fall out of harmony with the group, or they can sway our thinking to bring us in line with the group when we had previously disagreed with the prevailing wisdom.

The apostle Paul, a Pharisee, was a Jew from birth, educated and entrenched in Jewish law. In persecuting Christians, he was seeking to preserve that harmony he felt within the Jewish faith. Jewish high priests and governors of provinces sanctioned his actions as justified to maintain harmony in worship and the Jewish way of living. Paul had to be convinced dramatically with new information before he would or could change his attitude and begin to try to change the attitudes of others. The Acts of the Apostles chronicles this event on the road to Damascus.

> Meanwhile, Saul was still breathing out murderous threats against the Lord's disciples. He went to the high priest and asked him for letters to the synagogues in Damascus, so that if he found any there who belonged to the Way, whether men

> or women, he might take them as prisoners to Jerusalem. As he neared Damascus on his journey, suddenly a light from heaven flashed around him. He fell to the ground and heard a voice say to him, "Saul, Saul, why do you persecute me?"
>
> "Who are you Lord?" Saul asked.
>
> "I am Jesus, whom you are persecuting," he replied. "Now get up and go into the city, and you will be told what you must do."
>
> The men traveling with Saul stood speechless; they heard the sound but did not see anyone. Saul got up from the ground, but when he opened his eyes he could see nothing. So they led him by the hand into Damascus. For three days he was blind, and did not eat or drink anything.
>
> In Damascus there was a disciple named Ananias. The Lord called to him in a vision, "Ananias!"
>
> "Yes, Lord," he answered.
>
> The Lord told him, "Go to the house of Judas on Straight Street and ask for a man from Tarsus named Saul, for he is praying. In a vision he has seen a man named Ananias come and place his hands on him to restore his sight." (Acts 9:1–12)

The Scriptures tell us that after Paul had this profound awakening, Ananias followed the Lord's instruction and visited Paul, then known as Saul. "Then Ananias went to the house and entered it. Placing his hands on Saul, he said, 'Brother Saul, the Lord Jesus, who appeared to you on the road as you were coming here, has sent me so that you may see again and be filled with the Holy Spirit'" (Acts 9:17).

Paul was compliant and receptive to the idea that Jesus Christ is Lord. Submission has its rewards. Submit to the Word of God, and you will receive the gift of knowledge and the power to overcome.

The apostle then experienced a miracle. When Ananias laid hands on him, "Immediately, something like scales fell from Saul's eyes, and he could see again. He got up and was baptized, and after taking some food, he regained his strength" (Acts 9:18–19).

To be out of harmony with a group means that you are not in total agreement with everything the group presents or practices. This does not mean that you vehemently disagree and that you are withdrawing your complete support. However, once you are fully armed with knowledge, clear perception, memory, and judgment, you have the capacity to make a rational evaluation that may require you to break away from or align yourself with a cause, a person, or a group.

New attitudes change behaviors. Paul's experience changed his life in a most dramatic way. He made a 360-degree turn. All of our lives can be changed in the same way.

We can be changed completely by the Spirit of God. Paul underwent such change on the road to Damascus. Jesus Christ is God as part of the Trinity and can transfer His Spirit into anyone of His choosing.

He spoke to Paul on the road to Damascus, thus breathing the Holy Spirit upon him and changing him by this miracle. We often hear about this magnificent encounter, but we seldom reflect on its miraculous dimension.

Genesis 2:7 it tells us that "the Lord God formed the man from the dust of the ground and breathed into his nostrils the breath of life, and the man became a living being." Before doing this, the Lord God spoke to His counterparts, who were working with Him, and said, "Let us make man in our own image, in our likeness" (Genesis 1:26). Certainly He was speaking to Jesus Christ His Son and to the Holy Spirit.

So Jesus Christ was capable then and was even more capable after He had given His life for the redemption of mankind and had returned to heaven to be with the Father and was glorified by Him (Genesis 1:2, Job 26:13, Psalm 33:6, John 20:21–22).

The Spirit of God in Jesus Christ can transform us at any moment of our lives. To be out of harmony with the world should lead us into harmony with God. This logical step can change our lives for the better. Allowing ourselves to be transformed in and through Jesus Christ permits us to bring that same change to others who are in desperate need of healing. Others are depending on us to lead the way. Sometimes we are unaware of how much influence we have on our peers, who are following our every move. Let's make the right choice today!

Oh, the Chatter!

Are you guilty of talking so much that you miss important information that is being presented to you on a silver platter? If you are so busy talking, how do you know that you have missed an opportunity? Did someone point it out to you, or did you recognize this opportunity when only it was too late? We can certainly focus on our own chatter; however, chatter extends far beyond ourselves to include the environment in which we live, work, worship, and socialize.

Why do some of us talk so much that we miss the boat? Some of us refuse to show submission in our conversation. We want to demonstrate our strength and believe that to do anything contrary would render us weak according to society's dictates. In fact, this thinking may be the norm only in our small group. Still, our need to belong impels us to believe and to act in this manner.

Paul was totally convinced that his beliefs and actions were correct. He was a Pharisee, and those beliefs and actions were lawful because he had the backing of governors and high priests. But the Scriptures show that he was incorrect. Likewise, in our reluctance to listen, we demonstrate a belief that our views are the official standard by which everyone must exist. Everyone else must conform to share a relationship with us.

But life does not revolve around a few prevailing standards. Life is inclusive of all and should not be viewed in terms of societal constructs such as nation, state, county, parish, prefect, district, club, gender, class, age, or denomination. Life comes without restrictions and denials when we recognize and accept the supremacy and the loving grace of God through Jesus Christ.

Some of us have been shut out of worldly organizations because we have been judged unfit. Perhaps we did not have the right nationality, residence, education, wealth, gender, class, or religion. But with Jesus Christ, we need only be people whose hearts are pure, whose deeds are of light, and whose allegiance is to a God, our creator and our sustainer.

Paul wrote extensively later in life after having been retaught by the Holy Spirit. He said, "That is why, for Christ's sake, I delight in weaknesses, in insults, in hardships, in persecutions, in difficulties. For when I am weak, then I am strong" (2 Corinthians 12:10).

The Promised One has come and has laid down His life. He made the ultimate sacrifice for all of us. We are all the redeemed benefactors of undeserved grace. So though we are indeed weak, we are still strong.

This is not a contradiction. The true purpose of being in a submissive mode is to be able to reject the call to sin. To match action for action amounts to being as sinful as those baiting you with their evil deeds. Jesus Christ said, "The thief comes only to steal and kill and destroy" (John 10:10). The Lord added quite emphatically, "I have come that they may have life, and have it to the full."

Who Is the Thief?

The thief is any form of deceit affecting our lives. While someone we know may be full of deceit, we often cannot spot this quality until it becomes pronounced. By then it may be too late. That person may have subdued us by accusation, character assassination, or shaming before we realize his or her true nature. Material things can be so seductive in their beauty and their makeup that they capture our affections. We shrug off these feelings at first, but unchecked, they become worship. An idol has now been created in our lives. Idol worship is a sin, and that angers God.

The former angel of light who is now the Prince of Darkness has cunningly assembled a basket of temptations that we have accepted unawares. They have been delivered to us tied up with colorful ribbons.

He deals in all things of this earth and goes after all people. Some are immediately willing while others must be enticed with the things they covet. Either way, he recruits soldiers in his fight against God's people. They are mercenaries because they receive earthly pay in all sorts of material benefits from him. They are tricked into believing that there is no hell, that their heaven is here on earth, and that there are no consequences for what they do during their life's journey.

Jesus spoke to all who would listen to Him during his time here on earth, and He is still speaking through His recorded words in the Bible. He said many things during His ministry, even addressing those who refused to listen to Him. He said, "I tell you the truth, everyone who sins is a slave to sin" (John 8:34).

Those of us who have elected not to listen to God's Word and not to carry out His teachings have been unduly influenced by persons or things in our lives. We were all given the breath of life and the ability to think and to make decisions guided by the Spirit of God. However, some of us have been deceived by the renegade spirit of Satan, who uses people and things to entice and to capture his targets.

Satan deceives us with the things of this earth. Those things are already accessible to all men and women through the blessings of Jesus Christ and His heavenly Father. However, those things come with restrictions from God. Satan throws off the restrictions, convincing us that they are unnecessary and unimportant and that there are no consequences for ignoring them.

The Lord God created all of the elements of this earth, and they were all good in His sight. But human beings have combined or altered these things and used them in a manner contrary to the good of society. Some of these combinations or alterations bring great harm and pain as well as sinful pleasures. As a depraved mindset takes hold of a society, those not deeply rooted in God's laws succumb to temptation.

In John 8:43–44, Jesus Christ speaks to the dilemma of those who have been tricked by Satan. He presents the problem in the form of a question and then answers that question. He is deeply saddened when He sees us in a state of depravity. He speaks clearly to us, but some do not hear Him. Jesus says, "Why is my language not clear to you? Because you are unable to hear what I say" (John 8:43).

Jesus adds, "You belong to your father, the devil, and you want to carry out your father's desire. He was a murderer from the beginning, not holding to the truth, for there is no truth in him. When he lies, he speaks his native language, for he is a liar and the father of lies" (John 8:44). How much clearer could this explanation be? It comes from God Himself, the purveyor of all truths.

Thievery Will Attempt Your Overthrow

When Moses returned to Egypt with a mandate from God, he was continually rebuffed by Pharaoh until God was ready to release the Israelites from bondage in Egypt. That could not happen until the appointed time.

Before we examine the wonders God performed in Egypt, let us look at how Moses began his journey there. He visited his father-in-law Jethro and said, "Let me go back to my own people in Egypt to see if any of them are still alive" (Exodus 4:18). Jethro told him to go and wished him well on his journey.

Exodus 4:19 tells us, "Now the Lord had said to Moses in Midian, 'Go back to Egypt, for all the men who wanted to kill you are dead.'" That was a great reassurance to Moses! That should have bolstered his strength and eliminated his fears, especially given everything else the Lord had said and done to smooth his return to Egypt. "So Moses took his wife and sons, put them on a donkey and started back to Egypt. And he took the staff of God in his hand" (Exodus 4:20).

But we find out that Moses was still not completely convinced he could do the job laid out for him. The Lord had given him all of the assurances anyone could hope for and had equipped him with all that was needed to complete the task, but Moses continued to have doubts. He held the staff of God, which would allow him to do great miracles, but still he quivered with fear.

Sometimes adversity or even the possibility of trouble can deter a strong person, so consider the effects on someone who was caught up in self-doubt and who did not recognize his strengths. Consider the effects on someone whose self-worth has disintegrated. How about someone who has slipped to the bottom rung of society's ladder and who is trying to climb back up that ladder step by step while confronting adversity?

Where are you now? Are you still slipping, or are you trying to rebuild your self-esteem? Did you recently lose your job or your marriage, or does your problem involve your children? Did you lose a loved one, or are you battling an addiction? Maybe you are struggling with the question of who you are in this great universe and of your connection to its supreme ruler.

Who is He? Moses asked the questions that were important to him and got the answers. See Exodus 3:13–15.

The Lord God revealed to Moses that his task in Egypt would not be easy. God told Moses, "When you return to Egypt, see that you perform before Pharaoh all the wonders I have given you the power to do. But I will harden his heart so that he will not let the people go. Then say to Pharaoh, 'This is what the Lord says: Israel is my firstborn son, and I told you, "Let my son go, so he may worship me." But you refused to let him go; so I will kill your firstborn son'" (Exodus 4:21–23).

When the Lord said, "I will harden his heart so that he will not let the people go," He was declaring that Pharaoh would commit an act of willfulness sure to bring about a desired result. Pharaoh would refuse Moses, whom he saw as a nobody, in an attempt to thwart God's wishes. The arrogant king would bask in his strength as ruler of the vast Egyptian empire.

To Moses, this denial represented a challenge he was unwilling to face in his self-doubting condition. Hearing that Pharaoh's heart would be hardened into a state of resistance, Moses was taken back forty years when he had resisted the status quo, and what did it gain him? He had killed a man and had to flee Egypt into the desert! And now all this might end up with the killing of Pharaoh's firstborn son.

Moses didn't want to be involved if things were going to turn out this way. This indeed might be how most of us would respond to such a situation. Self-doubt is our enemy. What else could convince us that God's reassurances are not sufficient to sustain us? Only false knowledge could do this. "The fear of the Lord is the beginning of knowledge, but fools despise wisdom and discipline" (Proverbs 1:7).

Fear and self-doubt might have cost Moses his claim to greatness, his place in the history of humanity. The greatness of Moses was grounded in the greatness of God, and to conquer Moses would have been to conquer God. Evil is relentless in its attempts to strip the children of God of their just rewards and recognition. Moses was rescued thanks to the quick thinking of his wife, who knew of God's connectedness to the offering of blood.

How many times have we as sons and daughters of God and disciples of Jesus Christ thought and acted as Moses did when we realized that we would face challenges and delays? Aren't we just as equipped as Moses was when he left the mount of God?

I believe that we are even more equipped than he was. That is because we know of the coming and the sacrifice of Jesus Christ, who died for us and returned to heaven so that He could send the Holy Spirit to descend upon us. We have been doubly blessed in that we have been washed by the blood of Jesus and have been endowed with the Holy Spirit. With these blessings, we can do everything through Christ Jesus.

Moses was saved through the connectedness of the blood of circumcision and the covenant God had made with Abraham.

> Then God said to Abraham, "As for you, you must keep my covenant, you and your descendants after you for the generations to come. This is my

> covenant with you and your descendants after you, the covenant you are to keep: Every male among you shall be circumcised. You are to undergo circumcision, and it will be the sign of the covenant between me and you. For the generations to come every male among you who is eight days old must be circumcised, including those born in your household or bought with money from a foreigner—those who are not your offspring. Whether born in your household or bought with your money, they must be circumcised. My covenant in your flesh is to be an everlasting covenant. Any uncircumcised male, who has not been circumcised in the flesh, will be cut off from his people; he has broken my covenant." (Genesis 17:9–14)

We can credit Moses's wife Zipporah for understanding God's ways enough to have acted swiftly to save her husband's life. As Exodus 4:24–26 tells us, "At a lodging place on the way, the Lord met Moses and was about to kill him. But Zipporah took a flint knife, cut off her son's foreskin and touched Moses feet with it. 'Surely you are a bridegroom of blood to me,' she said. So the Lord let him alone. (At that time she said 'bridegroom of blood,' referring to circumcision.)"

We no longer rely on the blood of the foreskin. Moses was the bridegroom of blood to Zipporah, but a new and permanent Bridegroom was sacrificed, and his blood covers us all. He was beaten and scarred for twenty-two miles all the way to Calvary's mountain where He was nailed to a cross, and in His love, He dedicated in all of His suffering to us. Through His commitment of love, we are set free from all that attempts to rob, steal, and destroy us. Are you in Him today? Only through Jesus Christ can you fend off and defeat the thief who comes to rob, steal, and kill.

What thief is attempting to rob, steal, and destroy you? Is it the one who visited you when you were just a child, or is it the one who visited your parents. How about your former teacher or priest or that person who befriended you on the Internet? Who or what is it? You have tried so desperately to dismiss the memories. You have followed a path away from self-doubt and have made great strides. You have succeeded at higher education and have entered the corporate world, but just as you are ready to grasp everything you have strived for, the thief reappears.

You ask yourself, *What in the name of Jesus have I done to deserve this? I did everything in my power to set aside the pain and to move forward. Why now? I'm not the one who inflicted the pain. I have suffered from it and am still suffering, so why am I being made to remember it and to endure it again? It is not fair! I thought I was over this a long time ago. I do not understand why!*

Is this you? If so, what are you going to do to right this situation?

I want to remind you that the Bible tell us, "In the beginning God created the heavens and the earth" (Genesis 1:1). It tells us also that "the Lord God formed the man from the dust of the ground and breathed into his nostrils the breath of life, and the man became a living being" (Genesis 2:7). God is the first and only innovator. Before Him there was none, and still there is none who can equal His thoughts and His deeds. Because of Him everything good exists. To whom then shall we go?

Take your problems to God, who is your maker and your sustainer. He created us. He knows us intimately and can fix us whenever we are bruised, broken, and hurting. He was, still is, and will be forevermore. Don't be reluctant to reach for His powerful hand. Don't stand alone, waiting for a "burning bush" experience. That display was intended only for Moses, and since then God has changed His approach to convincing us to seek His help. No longer do we have to climb Mount Horeb to gain access to a loving and powerful God. He is available everywhere and any time! He provides multiple "burning bush" events in simple, everyday occurrences.

Begin to recognize and to acknowledge them! Hand everything over to God and leave it with Him. Don't go back and retrieve a problem just because you see no instantaneous movement. Trust God and He will take care of you.

Okay, so you are having trouble with the recognition and acknowledgment part. Approach God with humility, fearing His awesome power and recognizing the sacrifice He made for us in offering His only begotten Son. We are undeserving of this gift, but God came down from heaven as a man to redeem us from the failings of the first man, Adam, and from our own sins as well.

In Jesus Christ, who is God, we have a mediator and a representative of the Father. He does nothing on His own but consults with the Father, and so their decisions are in perfect union. Put your troubles into the river of crimson blood Jesus shed for you, and let them drift away. Trust that Jesus, who sits at the Father's right hand in heaven, is more than capable of shouldering your pains and disappointments. His death on the cross two thousand years ago made that possible, and this act does not have to be repeated every time you bring your troubles to Him. Once is forever!

Forever has no end, and God is endless in His love for us. Who else has made that commitment? No one else besides the Father and the Son! The Father sent Jesus Christ as His representative, and when you accept the Son, you accept the Father.

Perhaps you are still having trouble accepting that God wanted to kill Moses? The prophet was scared and was languishing in self-doubt. How could God contemplate such a thing?

In fact, God's anger was justified. After He had done everything necessary to fit Moses to return to Egypt, Moses doubted Him by doubting himself. Before he was in the womb, Moses had been chosen by God as the deliverer of the Hebrew people, who were in bondage in Egypt. He was born and reared for this task by God's love and grace. It was not just by happenstance that Moses was placed in a basket and sent floating down the Nile River and that the basket was guided to the spot in the river where Pharaoh's daughter was bathing. Every detail of Moses's life up to the point where he met God in the burning bush had been carefully orchestrated by God. So Moses's reluctance to accept his life's work angered God. In fact, the Scripture says that "God's anger burned against Moses" (Exodus 4:14).

We all have distinct purposes in life, and just as Moses had support in his wife Zipporah, each of us has support on this earth. The action taken by Zipporah to save her husband's life was rooted in the covenant God had made with Abraham through circumcision and blood. She quickly circumcised her son and touched the feet of Moses with the foreskin from that circumcision. Then she said, "Surely you are a bridegroom of blood to me" (Exodus 4:25). The Lord then gave Moses a reprieve, allowing him to live.

After Moses was granted this reprieve, he fulfilled his mission, delivering the children of Israel from bondage in Egypt. He did a splendid job in surmounting all of the challenges set before him, but he could not have accomplished any of this except by the power and the blessings of almighty God.

Is God's anger burning against you for any reason? If so, what support do you have for gaining a reprieve? Zipporah's demonstration tells us emphatically that the way to a reprieve is through God's covenant of blood. But today we no longer have to obtain this reprieve through circumcision, because we can rely on the sacrificial blood of Jesus of Nazareth. The old covenant has been replaced with eternal grace through the divine love of God the Father and Jesus Christ the Son. The only sacrifice we need to make to God is the eternal sacrifice of our hearts.

Once we have made this spiritual sacrifice through Jesus Christ, we ought to change our physical surroundings. We should seek a support system with viable mentors who will steer us in a heavenly direction. We want to be relieved of that earth-centered existence that can take us near heaven but no further. Certainly we can be happy only when we have reached heaven and are in the presence of God the Father, Jesus the Son, and the Holy Spirit.

Temptation Is Sin's Call to Human Nature

Jesus cursed a fig tree on his way into Jerusalem, and it immediately withered and died without producing any fruit. This is quite significant.

The Bible first mentions a fig tree in Genesis 3:7. Adam and Eve ate from the Tree of Knowledge of Good and Evil, and immediately their eyes were opened and they realized they were naked. Adam and Eve then took fig leaves and sewed them together to cover their nakedness.

There are more than a thousand varieties of fig trees, and some biblical researchers are convinced that the fruit Adam and Eve ate in the garden of Eden was actually the fruit of the fig tree, not of the apple tree, as we are led to believe.

When we commit sin, we wrap ourselves in secrecy, hoping it will cover us, but in fact we are naked as Adam and Eve were in the garden. They realized they were naked because of the truth of almighty God. He is all truth! The fig leaves they used to cover themselves were not enough, and God had to provide the skins of animals to properly cover their nakedness.

In the Middle East fig trees provide several crops of nourishing fruit each year in addition to supplying shade and firewood. In biblical times, dried figs were placed on strings and used as food for travel. Figs are high in protein and in carbohydrates and were used for long journeys across the desert where food was scarce.

Fig trees have an unusual way of becoming fruitful. The tree's edible fruit is called a syconium. This hollow structure is lined on the inside with hundreds of unisex flowers. A tiny female wasp enters the fruit through an opening in the syconium and pollinates the flowers inside. Ficus carica, the species found widely in the Middle East, produces edible fruit from the female trees only when the syconia are pollinated by this wasp.

Did Jesus know that the fig tree had no fruit? The Scripture says that it was not yet the season for fruit. So why was Jesus so hungry? Temptation is sin's call to human nature. Cursing the tree was Jesus's response to this temptation! He knew what was ahead, and He would not allow anything to get in the way. The second Adam came to do what the first Adam had failed to do—to conquer sin. To do that, He first had to do away with temptation, that great deception that was before Him.

Remember the temptation that Satan offered in the garden of Eden. Eve was deceived into believing that God's command regarding the Tree of Knowledge of Good and Evil was intended to prevent her and Adam from becoming gods themselves. Satan persuaded Eve that God was manipulating them to keep them in a docile state and that they would not die as God said. Genesis 3:6 says, "When the woman saw that the fruit of the tree was good for food and pleasing to the eye, and also desirable for gaining wisdom, she took some and ate it. She also gave some to her husband, who was with her, and he ate it."

In fact, when God told Adam that eating the fruit of the tree would bring death, He did not mean physical death but a spiritual death brought on by the loss of innocence. If we have lost our innocence, we must be guilty of sin. To disobey God is to sin, and that is what Satan caused Eve and Adam to do by eating the fruit and experiencing good and evil. Adam and Eve existed in an atmosphere of good before their encounter with Satan, and that was all they knew until that time. God created everything, and after surveying it, He determined that it was all good. Satan changed the tapestry of that magnificent existence by introducing Eve and Adam to the evil of sin, which brings alienation from God and the potential for eternal death and damnation.

America and the other great nations that are the leading producers of goods and services have evolved into marketing giants. Since we are constantly inventing and producing goods and services, we have to create markets of purchasers wherever they do not exist. We have convinced individuals, groups, and nations that everything we make is safe and essential to life.

Satan was a great marketer to Adam and Eve. He sold them on the merits of his completely deceptive campaign. He sold them a lemon, a product that does not live up to the claims made by the seller. Because Adam and Eve put their trust in Satan, humanity has fallen from a world where all was good into a world under the shadow of sin. "For all have sinned and fall short of the glory of God" (Romans 3:23). That is why Jesus Christ, the one true promise of redemption, entered this world. "For God so loved the world that he gave his one and only Son, that whoever believes in him shall not perish but have eternal life. For God did not send his Son into the world to condemn the world, but to save the world through him" (John 3:16–17).

So why did Jesus curse the fig tree? Because He knew that temptation is deception and manipulation, which leads to sin.

Satan, the tempter, the deceiver, and the ardent propagator of sin, knew full well why the Son of God had come down from heaven. Satan was no stranger to God, for he was a resident of heaven held in high regard until he rebelled against God. After losing the battle to take over the kingdom of heaven, Satan received his just due and was thrown out of heaven along with all of the angels who had been deceived by him and had participated in this rebellion. In his quest for power and equality with God, Satan has set his sights on the domination of the people of God on earth. He has set himself up as ruler pro tem of earth as well as the terrestrial and celestial lower heavens.

After his banishment from heaven, Satan took on the title of the Prince of Darkness. He became the chief opponent of peace and of the children of God. Satan has been quite busy in attempting to block God's children from ascending through righteousness into heaven to be with God for eternity. He is our nemesis on the journey of faith. Satan is bent on destroying all the people of this world. Through deception, trickery, and manipulation of the truth, he hopes to bring about the debilitation and then the eternal death of God's people.

If we intend to reach a destination, our directions ought to be correct and precise. Let's say that we were given a map but it did not depict details of the area we were trying to reach or it showed a different city, county, or state than the one we wanted. We would be lost until we could get proper directions.

Some of us would backtrack and after reaching our point of origin would seek the right directions and take another stab at the journey. Less determined travelers would plan the trip for a later date. Finally, some would give up on the trip and complain about the gross inconvenience they had encountered in their only attempt.

In all of these situations, Satan has had an influence on people's lives. God gives us challenges, but He does this not to see us fail but to expand our faith and wisdom. Satan, who wishes us to remain uninformed about his diabolical schemes, will cause us to fail. We treat many failings in life as innocent mistakes, never understanding that Satan is working through persons or things to cause these missteps, misjudgments, and missed opportunities.

This father of lies is crafty and full of deceit and will persuade you to blame God for his devilish deeds. He will tell you that God has forgotten you or does not love you. He will pierce your heart bit by bit until he controls it, all the while comforting you with the false promise that he will love you, that he will provide all your needs, and that he is the true God.

After he pulls you close, seeming to love and to cherish you, he will devour you just as a spider draws its prey into a web and devours it. The loving and cherishing appear to be gifts, but such gifts come in unholy wrappings. After enjoying such gifts for a while, you are conditioned to desire them all the time. You are now a convert to darkness, not even realizing that your light has slipped away.

If you and I are in the first group that backtracked and quickly got accurate directions to our destination, we have little or no room for discouragement. We will mount up again and take the right road with purpose. We have made up our minds that we won't be denied. We need to have purpose in our lives, and our directions must be in line with our purpose. Appearing to be in line, or being close to it, is not good enough, because this will not bring us to our destination. If we are thrown off course, we will suffer doubt, mistrust, insecurity, fatigue, and defeat.

Recognizing those times when we are thrown off course through sinful subterfuge is the key to winning, because then we can step up our worship and praise of the God who sends us help. He utters His commands in our defense, and His words are a lamp that lights the way for our feet and graces our pathways with light in the midst of darkness (Psalm 119:105).

Keeping our eyes on the prize requires that we first recognize that there is a glorious prize to be had and that it is at the end of the journey and not at the beginning or in the middle. Our God worked for the first six days of creation before resting on the seventh day, and He expects us to do the same. In fact, He commanded us to do that, so why should we think that we are exempt from making an effort to reach our destination? God gives us directions to reach our righteous destination, but if we do not know Him and have a relationship with Him, how can we achieve what He intends? Those directions will go unheeded or unused.

God gave us directions, but He still speaks to and guides us day by day, so if we are not communing with Him we will miss out on the timely directives that address every situation in our lives. We must find him now! He is easy to locate, and once we find Him we must stay close to Him. He is always waiting for us. If we have postponed the trip after the first attempt with the erroneous directions, we shouldn't get complacent and lackadaisical to the point that we never seek to find the right path to the prized destination. Satan is busy seeking whom he can devour, so we ought to guard our hearts and minds and spirits. How can we do this if we have not put on the breastplate of righteousness?

God ordained his prophets to foretell the coming of Jesus Christ and to proclaim His mission, but the great deceiver had widely influenced the thinking of many to believe a lie. He had them thinking that Jesus Christ would come to lead the people into a battle against Roman rule, to overthrow the Roman Empire, and to free Israel.

Satan blinded many people to the true mission of Jesus. Consider the mindset of Herod in Matthew's gospel regarding his kingship over the territory where Jesus was born. He sought to kill the baby Jesus before he had a chance to become the king of the Jews. If Jesus was to be the king of the Jews, Herod feared that he would be ousted from office or even killed, perhaps along with all of his heirs and his family.

Herod moved swiftly in reaction to this deception, committing great sins as he slaughtered countless children in hopes of eliminating this perceived threat to his kingship and his dynasty. Jesus survived this attempted murder at the hands of Herod, who was under Satan's influence. When Jesus began His ministry, Satan decided to challenge Him in person, because Jesus Christ had to be vanquished before He could complete the mission of restoring God's people through grace. So, after He was baptized in the Jordan River by John, Jesus was led away into the desert by the Spirit to be tempted by the Devil (Matthew 3, 4).

Jesus was not left unprotected by His Father in this face-off with Satan. As with their first confrontation in heaven, holiness and good won over temptation and deception, and would win again and again in the person of Jesus Christ. "As soon as Jesus was baptized, he went up out of the water. At that moment heaven was opened, and he saw the Spirit of God descending like a dove and alighting on him. And a voice from heaven said, 'This is my Son, whom I love; with him I am well pleased'" (Matthew 3:16–17).

As Jesus was led away into the desert, He began a fast that lasted forty days and forty nights. Jesus was also hungry later in His ministry when He saw the fig tree on His way into Jerusalem. (See Matthew 21 and Mark 11.) Because Satan knew that the Lord had not eaten for this long period in the desert, he began to tempt the physical man Jesus as he did Adam and Eve in the garden. Satan does this to us every day, mostly at our weakest points. Satan declared to Jesus, "If you are the Son of God, tell these stones to become bread" (Matthew 4:3). Jesus is God and not subject to Satan's will. Jesus had the power to curse this temptation and to render it null and void, and He did just that. Jesus answered, "It is written: 'Man does not live on bread alone, but on every word that comes from the mouth of God'" (Matthew 4:4).

Jesus had entered Jerusalem the evening before He cursed the fig tree in Bethany. After He had gone to the temple and looked around, He decided to return to Bethany since it was already late. In the morning when He was journeying back to Jerusalem, the temptation of hunger came upon Him just as when He was in the desert and was tempted by Satan. Jesus had cursed that hunger before, so in cursing the fig tree, He was reinforcing what He had done and reiterating His power over sin and Satan.

Satan tempted Jesus with hunger when He was beginning His mission of redeeming God's people. Jesus was now starting the final chapter of His ministry, looking to complete what He had begun in the name of the Father. Satan attempted to bog Him down in the concerns of the flesh so that Jesus would be derailed from the plan He was setting out to complete.

How many times have you committed yourself to start or to complete a task or to fix a situation that has been left hanging and suddenly found your mind has been changed? You have wavered, procrastinated, and in some cases decided to do nothing because you felt that the situation no longer demanded your attention and that you could leave it to someone else. But as soon as you adopted this attitude, everything began to blow up right before your eyes. If only you had taken the right steps in the first place this mess could have been avoided.

Jesus had to return to Jerusalem to reclaim God's temple for Himself and for His Father. He had to rid the temple of the money changers and of the buyers and the sellers who were perpetrating thievery in the name of God. In cursing the fig tree, He rejected the temptation of Satan, who tried to obstruct Him so that He could not prepare the temple. In preparing the temple in Jerusalem, the city of God, Jesus would allow Himself to be in the designated place to be the sacrificial Lamb that provided the cleansing blood.

As God the Father shed the blood of animals to cover the sinful bodies of Adam and Eve, Jesus the sacrificial Lamb had to be crucified to cover the sins of humanity. Blood was shed in the garden of Eden to cover the nakedness of Adam and Eve after they were deceived by Satan, and now Jesus Christ had to sacrifice Himself to provide covering for our spiritual nakedness. Adam and Eve tried to cover their nakedness and their sins with the leaves of the fig tree, but these leaves weren't enough. Fig leaves and the blood of lambs, rams, goats, bulls, and doves could not cover our sins before God. Thus Jesus Christ had to shed His blood to cover us all.

Though the fig tree was bursting with green leaves, it had no edible fruit. Deception is always at our doors, and we must be able to recognize it at all times and put it behind us as we continue to move forward in the Spirit of God. For God created us to be apart from sin. So what was it in human nature that allowed us to be so vulnerable to temptation?

Ignorance and disobedience of authority allowed this to happen! Eve chose to abandon God's commands at a mere suggestion from Satan that what God said was not so (Genesis 3:1–5). In her abandonment of authority, Eve fell victim to the lies that corrupted humanity and stopped it short of God's glory. At that moment self-deception and self-destruction became her companions. Adam was alone in the garden of Eden, so God created Eve as a suitable companion. We humans share with our companions, and as a companion Eve did the obvious with the fruit that she had just eaten: she shared it with Adam.

What will we share with our companions? If we have been duped and led astray, will we seek to do the same to our friends? Or will we stop and take stock of what has happened to us and hope that our friends will not be subjected to this same deception? Will we then enlighten and protect them from these same abuses by Satan?

The parable of the sower tells us about a person who sowed many seeds and about the different places and conditions where the seeds were sown. Some seeds survived and began to grow, but for some reason they died and did not produce fruit. But some seeds were deposited in good soil and fared wonderfully, returning sixty and one hundred fold. The parable speaks about fruit that is good for the soul, the Word of God being sown in the hearts of men. But we should also remember that some seeds bear poisonous fruits.

What kind of seeds are you sowing and what kind of fruits are you eating? Are you planting seeds that produce poison that you are distributing to the unsuspecting and the uninformed? If you are this type of farmer, take note that Jesus Christ will judge you as being destructive and a hindrance to His people, whom you have led astray. He will sentence you to the lake of eternal fire for every soul that has been damned because of you. It will be bad enough that you have to answer for yourself. Just think how much harder the punishment will be for each soul added to your account of temptation and deception.

It is far better to be the sower of good seed. God's words are steadfast and supreme, never losing their authority. This world may pass away, but God's words will survive. The only way of surviving with God is to grasp His Son, Jesus Christ. He is the only one who can rescue the perishing. As the song goes, "He cares for the dying. He snatches them in pity from sin and the grave" (Fannie J. Crosby, "Rescue the Perishing"). Jesus Christ is able to undo the wrongs you have done with His power to forgive, but why do wrong when you can avoid being deceived? Jesus Christ can curse the fig trees in all of our lives and cause them to wither without producing the fruit of destruction.

Generational Things

God's wrath has been poured out on humanity because the world has hidden His Word of Truth in a barrel. Some of us try to keep a lid on that barrel all of our lives, and some of us place this lid on the barrel when we want our own way, no matter what. We want to do our own thing and to be in complete charge of our lives, and we will accept no restrictions. So who can pass judgment on others? No one! We are all guilty. Can the pot call the kettle black? Some of us are jumping out of the frying pan and seeking refuge in the fire below (Romans 1:18–19)._God has made all things plain to humanity, beginning with Adam and Eve, but like them, we have swept the truth under the rug while we revel in darkness and lies.

The human race has an Adamic nature. We quickly assign blame as did Adam. Confronted by the Lord, he said Eve had caused him to disobey God's command. In eating the fruit from the Tree of Knowledge of Good and Evil, Adam and Eve denied the truth of God's authority. In rejecting this authority over their lives, they glorified darkness. They took on sin in accepting the serpent's words over those of God (Romans 1:21).

The people of Nimrod's time wanted to see what God was doing in heaven and worked to set up their own government in opposition to the Lord's kingdom. To make a name for themselves, they were building a tower that would stretch all the way to heaven, so God dispersed them. What darkness lurks in the hearts of men! The people in the time of Noah had to be erased from the living. The children of Israel rebelled against Moses and God in the desert, and they carried their opposition to authority into the land of milk and honey. And this spirit of rebellion and sin continue in us today. We are all guilty! Read Romans 3:23.

Romans 1:21 tells us that although our forefathers knew God, they failed to glorify Him and to give Him thanks. We have failed in the same way. We humans have great memories, but if we have not used information for a prolonged period, we will forget it completely or in part. We will remember simple multiplication like 2 x 2 = 4 unless we suffer an accident to the brain that wipes out all information. But if we have been away from the daily grind of the classroom for a long time, we will not remember how to solve a geometry, algebra, trigonometry, or calculus problem. We have not used this information in years. In the same way, we forget the Word of God by not using it or failing to acknowledge Him.

Those who forgot God and His ways are given over to their own sinful desires. All of their thinking becomes futile. They believe they are wise, but they prove to be fools. They exchange the truth of God for lies. This process began with Adam and Eve and it continues today.

Those who suppress the truth do not think it worthwhile to retain the knowledge of God, so He gives them over to a depraved mind to do the things that they ought not to do. They become filled with depravity, greed, murder, strife, deceit, malice, gossip, and slander. These God-haters are insolent, arrogant, boastful, senseless, faithless, heartless, and ruthless, and they invent ways to do evil. The saddest part is that those who know that the end of all this ungodliness is death encourage others to do these things by continuing to do them themselves and approve of the like behavior of those they have influenced (Romans 1:28–32).

Do not be influenced by these people. They lead only to death. But Jesus brought light to this world!

We humans want to belong, to be heard and seen, to be accepted, and to be held in esteem, but we must not make the wrong choices to obtain what we are seeking. Sometimes we do not know what is best for us. Darkness may creep in unannounced, leaving us unsure or confused about the right position to take. We should not try to please society by choosing what is popular. Society may be going down an immoral path. We humans have the breath of God within us, and the Holy Spirit, sent through the death and resurrection of Jesus Christ, is always available to us. We ought to stop for consultation before we leap in head first, grasping at everything that gratifies the flesh.

Seeking only to satisfy the flesh suppresses the spirit and locks out God's light, which was provided through the blood of the crucified Jesus Christ. We should always ask God about our choices before we act and risk self-condemnation.

Yes, we have an Adamic nature, but we can break free of the seduction of sin by recognizing and accepting Jesus Christ. He is the truth and the light that shines along the way to salvation. Only He can sanctify us through His death and resurrection and free us from our generational course of destruction.

When Good Intentions Come with a But

I am sure there have been times when you were certain that the things you were attempting were right for you and that you were doing them in the right way and at the right time. But even with that confidence these efforts were unrewarding or in some cases disastrous. We have all had those experiences. We sometimes begin with success and continue on without consulting the manual until problems arise. Some of us will not seek help until disaster strikes. Sometimes we are deceived into thinking that our good intentions will suffice and that we will conquer all odds, but we don't.

Deceptions are quite common, and over time even the most learned people become convinced that they are hearing the truth, the answers for our times. The young are eager to conform to new ways of thinking, and the older generation is ready to tweak Christian norms to accommodate waywardness. We will hold a vote if necessary to make our sinfulness law so we can continue doing as we please. We will even use quotes from the Bible to justify our behavior. Some say that our God is a loving God and that they are acting in the spirit of love and should not be condemned. But woe to those who intentionally or even unintentionally deceive by labeling their sins as truth.

The information age has made this quite easy. The Internet and social media outlets are forums for pushing sinful views and lifestyles and influencing norms and mores. We should use these tools carefully.

Most people continue to seek the psychological support derived from religion. They may not do so regularly, but they will often turn to religion in times of uncertainty and disaster. Look at how Americans came together after the 9/11 terror attacks. People of many faiths united to worship and to pray for safety and peace.

Social norms are more often dictated by the media than by the church. We say that we want government out of our lives. We also don't want our lives to be controlled by the church, by priests or by pastors. We will make the decisions for ourselves!

The church, which once had great authority over human behavior, has been compromised by malfeasance, misjudgment, inaction, and revisionist teaching. How can the church regain control? Can this happen when some in the church preach deceptive doctrine? Churches that do not confront sin are filled. They preach tolerance as the main portal to salvation but leave damnation unexplored. Such ministries prefer not to mention hell since prosperity and living the good life here on earth are their main themes. Those of you accustomed only to this type of preaching need to know that an alternative exists.

Certain factions of the church have pulled a Charlie Gordon (*Flowers for Algernon*) on themselves and their congregations. They were not comfortable with preaching the unadulterated gospel and allowing congregations to rise and fall in a natural manner. In their desire to increase numbers in the pews along with the financial bottom line, they took drastic steps to make noticeable changes. Some abandoned the old hymns and adopted all genres of contemporary music. The messages have been flowery and without substance. Clergy and church administrators are happy with the numbers and the finances. They are convinced that they have found a way to have better worship and an improved relationship with

God. They think they have succeeded when in truth the drastic steps they have taken have been a failed experiment with dramatic side effects. Regression of souls is inevitable.

I have no objection to contemporary music in the church because many of those contemporary songs are bringing souls to Christ. They wash over me and create a desire to worship more, and I continue to bask in the infinity of God's love and grace. So I know the effects of these songs on others, especially younger worshipers. However, some contemporary songs mimic almost completely the music of the world except for a few word changes. Some songs never mention God or Jesus, sin or death. They may allude to a higher power, but they never speak His name.

The musical arrangements, beats, and singing of some songs are what you would hear in clubs, bars, and other social hangouts. But if there is nothing specific that the dancers can hold on to besides having a good time, what was it all for? Sure, we know that artists have to support themselves and have to consider the financial aspects of their careers. But in the end, churches must make better choices.

Some will say that we have to entice people to come to church before we will have the opportunity to convert them, so we should ply them with familiar things in the hope that eventually they will be changed. But we can't convert anyone. That is the job of the Holy Spirit. We have to provide the right diet so that spiritual persons are nurtured. The Holy Spirit will bring about the harvest after the ground has been plowed and the seeds have been planted and tended to.

When you build a house of God on a foundation of sand, it will eventually crumble. The building will stand in its magnificence for all to admire for a long time, but people's souls will travel down a slippery slope and will be lost forever if there is no intervention and correction.

There was a rich man who lived opulently and ate sumptuously while another man lived in squalor and hunger. If you have been reading your Bible or hearing the right kind of preaching, you will recognize this as the opening of a story told by Jesus Christ in the New Testament.

If you have never read or heard the story, I challenge you to find it and read it for yourself. Your unbelief could be changed by this parable. Hell has a prominent place in the Scriptures, and our Lord does not want us to end up there. God created hell, and He knows its horrible atrociousness and its unfathomable pain and suffering. In addition to all of those things there is complete isolation and darkness without end. There is no escaping hell. Once you have been sentenced to hell, you will stay there for eternity. Why, then, would you choose to be ignorant of such a possibility?

The Scriptures tell of Noah, Moses, Isaiah, Jeremiah, Ezekiel, Daniel, Hosea, Joel, Amos, Obadiah, Jonah, and many more prophets. I challenge you to read the Bible and to find out what the Lord God had them to say to us. They spoke to the world to come as well as to the world of old. They spoke to all of God's children. We have had more than enough people of God speaking to us in the here and now, so if someone wound up in hell and was able to return to warn us of this eternal disaster, would we believe this person? We would certainly not believe him, because we would tell ourselves, *If he has escaped to tell us about hell, it must not be that bad. If I wind up in hell, I too am learned, skillful, crafty, and personable enough to escape.*

But the truth is this: no one can escape and come back to the living. God created a divide to keep us out of hell. He made hell for rebellious angels, not for us, but since some of us have followed the chief rebel, Satan the deceiver, we will dwell with him in his eternal domain.

At this point some of you may be saying to yourselves, *I chose this book because of the title and did not expect scary topics like hell and damnation. I was looking for a light and airy self-help book, something to build my self-esteem and my determination for success.* Keep reading because God's words and direction are exactly what you need to succeed.

God breathed life into you at the beginning, and later He gave you the benefit of the Holy Spirit. He saw the suffering produced because of the deceiver, and He sent His only Son, Jesus Christ, and the Holy Spirit so that we would not only have life but would have it more abundantly (John 3:16).

Maybe you are in a valley of hurt and despair, but remember that you are not alone. Many have cried before you, and many are crying now, but help is always available for the asking. Jesus stands at the door knocking, and if you open the door He will come in and attend to you (Revelation 3:20).

Take heart in the knowledge that great men of the Bible have also cried, so you are in good company. Abraham cried and so did Jacob, Joseph, David, Jonathan, Elisha, Hezekiah, Ezra, Nehemiah, Job, Peter, Paul, John, Isaiah, and even Jesus Christ, our Lord and Savior. So cry, but do it in the fullness of His knowledge. Cry out to Him who is able to do immeasurably more than we can ask or imagine (Ephesians 3:20–21).

I cry too. In fact, I weep openly when the Holy Spirit awakes His indwelling in me and anoints me to do His work.

The Lord God can do all good things in you, and He does them according to His power working in you. He brings you good things from all of His riches. Believe it! It is so!

We Struggle with Ill-Conceived Plans

"I have seen it done that way." "I have a plan that I think will solve the problem and accomplish what I intend to do." With these self-assured words, we set about our tasks. We have the best of intentions and work hard to organize and to carry out our plans, but we forget to share them with God, to ask His opinion, and to seek His help. If we do not consult someone of such paramount importance in all of our lives, why should we be disappointed when things fall apart?

The greatest thinker who ever lived outside of Jesus Christ said, "What has been will be again, what has been done will be done again; there is nothing new under the sun" (Ecclesiastes 1:9). People have been making the same mistakes we are making today for ages. King David, whom Scriptures call a man after God's heart, sought the Lord on almost every occasion he did something. He had an ongoing relationship with God that blossomed as if it existed in an everlasting spring. But the few times he chose to keep God out of the equation he paid the price in his failures or had to endure the guilt of someone else's demise in these ventures.

Some of us rely on science and ignore the fact that science was created only through God's goodness. We set out not only to solve scientific issues but to disprove God's existence. Many flatly deny His existence and aptly label themselves as atheists. Not only have they denied God, but they have denied the existence of good and evil, of heaven and hell. The greatest scientists have God to thank for their discoveries. Satan, who always works against God, influences the scientists who try to debunk the Bible and all that supports God's creation of the universe and of its creatures, man included.

Can any man disprove God? Absolutely not! He will only succeed in his own destruction and that of the people who join in such a farce. If you are pondering the Darwinian theory, the big bang theory, or any others, look to the Bible as a valid source in your investigations.

God is supernatural and is above supernatural things. Therefore, man cannot fully explain Him. Consider this story from the Bible. The feat is explainable in today's technological age but remains outside of the realm of man.

David had just been anointed king of Israel, meaning both Judah and Jerusalem. The Philistines, Israel's archenemies, heard of this development and immediately set out to kill him. David had caused a huge stain on their history when he was just a shepherd boy. After he had been anointed by the prophet Samuel as Israel's king in waiting, David went to the battlefront where Israel's army was in a standoff against the Philistine army. There the lad killed the Philistines' greatest warrior and hero, Goliath. He did this through the anointing of God and turned the tide of the battle.

The Israelite army under the leadership of King Saul had been frozen in fear for forty days because of the obstacle that stood before them, Goliath, the giant warrior. David removed that obstacle so the Israelites could move forward. David would not become king for many years. Saul refused to abdicate until he was killed in battle. But now, because of the memory of David's bravery against them, the Philistines wanted to eliminate him before he grew even stronger and caused Israel to be even greater. The Philistines gathered in full force for battle and searched for David. He went out to meet the Philistine army, but after hearing that the enemy had already struck a blow against Israel, attacking the valley of Rephaim, David inquired of God, "Shall I go and attack the Philistines? Will you hand them over to me?" God answered, "Go, I will hand them over to you" (1 Chronicles 14:10).

The first confrontation took place at Baal Perazim. The Philistines fled and abandoned their gods. Though David and the Israelite army had won a victory, the Philistines regrouped and attacked again. David asked God whether he should respond in kind to this new attack. Once again God answered David. Note the relevance of including God in every part of our lives. God gave a detailed answer and presented a miraculous plan. Before I lay out that plan, I pause to ask these questions. Who is the greatest strategist in our lives? Who is the greatest leader in our lives? Who is the greatest victor in our lives? God is in every case!

God told David, "Do not go straight up, but circle around them and attack them in front of the balsam trees. As soon as you hear the sound of marching in the tops of the balsam trees, move out to battle, because that will mean God has gone out in front of you to strike the Philistine army" (1 Chronicles 14:14–15). When we call on God and his true representative, Jesus Christ, we can be certain that a plan will be laid out for us and that victory is assured. God does not just offer plans, He goes out before us or sends His emissaries, the angels.

"So David did as God commanded him, and they struck down the Philistine army, all the way from Gibeon to Gezer. So David's fame spread throughout every land, and the Lord made all the nations fear him" (1 Chronicles 14:16–17).

It is impossible for human soldiers to march on treetops, so detractors will say that this is not a believable story, though it is. Some may say that audio devices were installed in the treetops and that they were used to instill fear in the Philistine army, which couldn't have expected the sound of marching in the trees. Even if the Israelites used such a trick, it was quite ingenious. In that era, it certainly would have been inventive. But let's look at a modern battle involving the nation of Israel and surrounding Arab states. This battle ended in the defeat of Israel's enemies in a way remarkably similar to David's defeat of the Philistines.

In 1967 Israel was attacked by its neighbors. Israel defeated its enemies and recaptured lands that it had lost previously. Israel's air force ruled the skies, and the Arab forces were no match for its mechanized battalions. Israel's soldiers were well trained and ready for any such attack, but these advantages may not have been the decisive factor. Many thousands of enemy soldiers abandoned their weapons small and large. Some ran away while others waited for the Israelis and begged for mercy at their arrival.

When these enemy soldiers were asked by the Israelis why they had given up their arms, they offered stunning responses. They reported hearing a roar of tanks and armor that they had never heard before. They testified to seeing hundreds of Israeli tanks. Some said they had seen many angels fighting along with the Israeli army. Such sights and sounds terrified them to the point of surrender. Israel vanquished all of its enemies in six days. Thus history records this as the Six-Day War. Again, God did supernatural things in Israel. He still does these things in the lives of people who obey Him. Please take special note!

"Where there is no revelation, the people cast off restraint; but blessed is he who keeps the law" (Proverbs 29:18).

"My people are destroyed from lack of knowledge. Because you have rejected knowledge, I also reject you as my priests; because you have ignored the law of your God, I also will ignore your children" (Hosea 4:6).

Acting without God

I have demonstrated what happens when we maintain a relationship with God and consult Him about all of our actions. Now I will explore an action taken by King David without consultation and reliance on God's instructions. I will begin by looking at 1 Chronicles 13.

King David wanted to move the ark of God from Kiriath Jearim to Jerusalem, the city of God. The ark had been captured by the Philistine army just before King Saul's reign. No, God cannot be captured! But He allowed His ark to be taken by the Philistines to show His disappointment in His people the Israelites. They were disobedient and engaged in sinful behavior. God also wanted to inflict a penalty on the Philistines for their continued campaigns against Israel and to let them know that He was the true God of all. For this account, go to 1 Samuel 5, 6.

The Philistines placed the ark in their temple in Ashdod before their god Dagon. God then destroyed Dagon piece by piece. They were gripped with fear and moved the ark to another city, and God inflicted everyone in that city with tumors. The Philistines sent the ark to yet another city, but the people cried out against it being there, saying, "Send it back to Israel." It was returned to Israel but not without further incident.

The Philistines worshiped a false god, and even when the ark was placed in the temple with dire results for Dagon, they still were not completely convinced that their god was worthless. When they decided to send away the ark, they consulted their false prophets and holy men about how to do this. The answers they gave were not correct because these men had no knowledge of God's instructions to Moses when the ark was built. They did not know how it should be handled and transported or who should care for it.

Determined to free themselves of the ark, the Philistines made a cart of wood, hitched it to two cows that had borne calves, and placed the ark upon it. They made gold objects as a guilt offering, but this offering was rooted in the occult and in magic practice. They watched the cart to see whether the cows would follow the path into the Israelite territory of Beth Shemesh. If they did, the Philistines would be convinced that the God of Israel was behind the sufferings inflicted on them. If the cart returned to their territory, they would be convinced that it was not the God of Israel who caused their calamities.

The cart entered Beth Shemesh, and the inhabitants were exhilarated that the ark had returned to them. The cart came to a stop by a rock in the field of Joshua of Beth Shemesh while they were harvesting wheat in a valley. The Levites immediately took the ark down from the cart along with the golden objects and placed them on the rock. Then they chopped up the wooden cart and used it to make a fire to offer sacrifices to the Lord God. They sacrificed the two cows as burnt offerings and continued celebrating until some of them got overzealous and looked into the ark. They had brought on sorrows. No one could look into the ark of God. It was forbidden!

God killed seventy men instantly. When God forbids something, He means it regardless of our intentions, so it pays to consult the manual before installation or assembly. The people of God were dealt a harsh blow, so much so that they began to ask a familiar question, "Who can stand in the presence of the Lord, his holy God?" (1 Samuel 6:20). Psalm 24 offers a distinct answer to this question.

Jesus Christ stood in the place of God because He was His Son, sinless, full of light, full of love, and holy. He was and still is the only one able to do this. He is worthy!

The people of Beth Shemesh sent messengers to Kiriath Jearim telling the people there that the ark had been returned and that they should take it, and so the men of Kiriath Jearim came down and transported the ark to the house of Abinadab. Eleazar and his son were consecrated to guard the ark, which remained there until Israel became a nation governed by kings. Saul was chosen by God and anointed by the prophet and judge Samuel as the first king, but he later ran afoul of God and was rejected by Him. David was chosen by God to replace Saul and was anointed. He awaited Saul's abdication, but Saul would not leave the throne. Finally, Saul was killed in battle and David was installed as king. Now he set out to bring the ark to Jerusalem, something neither Saul nor the people of Kiriath Jearim had attempted to do.

In his haste to do something good, David conferred with his officers, his commanders, and the assembly of Israel, saying that if it was pleasing to them and was the will of God, he would send word far and wide to people in all the territories to join in returning the ark to Jerusalem. So David gathered all of Israel and journeyed to Kiriath Jearim in celebration. They brought the ark out from the house of Abinadab and placed it on a new cart with two men, Uzzah and Ahio, guiding the cart. As they brought the ark outside, they all made a joyful noise, led by the king in worship and in celebration of God's presence and glory. However, during all this time David never consulted with God directly. He simply said, "If it is the will of the Lord our God."

David had not consulted God to find out if the method used by the Philistines to transport the ark was the correct one, who should be the caretakers of the ark, what specific precautions should be taken in handling it, and who should be responsible for lifting and placing it. What should they do to ensure that God was not offended? There was no consultation at all. So even though they were well intentioned and full of zeal, David and his party were bound to make unintended mistakes and to incur God's wrath.

As the oxen were drawing the cart carrying the ark, they stumbled, knocking the cart off balance and causing the ark to shift. Uzzah reached out and touched the ark, attempting to steady it, but no one could touch the ark and live. Uzzah was killed instantly by God. He is pure and holy and without sin. He is righteous in all of His facets and will not allow Himself to be contaminated by sinfulness. As men and women with the nature of Adam and Eve, we have all sinned and have bathed ourselves in unrighteousness. God was angered that such unrighteousness had made direct physical contact with Him who is holy and righteous, so He purged it instantaneously.

Without righteousness we cannot see and be with God in His kingdom. Without God we cannot succeed as we were meant to do and will always fall short of the glory we could have had with Him through the acceptance of His sacrificed Son, Jesus Christ.

David was thrown off balance by this occurrence, but above all he was frightened of God, because he knew that he had not consulted Him as he should have done. David was responsible for Uzzah's death. Realizing his mistake and not wishing to add to the disaster, he decided to leave the ark at the house of Obed-Edom the Gittite while he inquired of the Lord. David then asked the question he should have asked the Lord before he began the quest to transport the ark: "How can I ever bring the ark of God to me?" (1 Chronicles 13:12).

After David asked the question, the answer was revealed to him and he began new preparations prescribed by God Himself. The Levites had been designated by God to be priests, the holy men of Israel. They were consecrated for the work of God by Moses, who had delivered the Israelites from captivity in Egypt. It was their task to carry the ark of God.

David summoned the Levites and owned up to his mistake, which had drawn down God's anger on the people. He asked the

Levites to consecrate themselves to the task of carrying the ark as prescribed with the designated poles resting on their shoulders. Everything was arranged according to the details that God had given Moses in the desert, and the procession to Jerusalem took on a new jubilation (1 Chronicles 15).

Are you constantly struggling with everything you do? Is this because you have not allowed yourself to trust in the unseen God? Surely you believe in something or many things, and yet you struggle with the idea that He exists and that He is not seen in the flesh. How can you believe in someone you cannot see? In fact, God can be found in all aspects of your life if you know how to recognize Him. He gave you life, and no one else could do this. Your parents created you in a biological act, but it was God who created the method and the bodies capable of completing this miraculous feat.

We exist in an environment that continually provides morning, afternoon, evening, and night. How about spring, summer, fall, and winter? We also have dew, rain, snow, hail, thunder, winds, lightning, and the sun. Who made them? What about the stars, the planets, the moons, and the air you breathe? Besides your parents and other family members, who protects you from harm and death? Even the most knowledgeable persons can never comprehend God's width, breadth, height, or depth.

Job suffered quite a lot in his lifetime, but he also knew God's love and might quite intimately. Because of this knowledge and because of their relationship, God surrounded him with much protection and success. After boasting about Job's faith and commitment, God was challenged by Satan to withdraw the protection He had placed around Job as a reward for his righteousness. Satan is always challenging God in so many ways. Are you being challenged by Satan because of God's protection and love for you? Perhaps in your trials you don't recognize this to be so. Though Job endured devastation of body and mind, God protected the most valuable part of him, his spirit. He is doing the same for you!

In the end, the tempter and the tester failed in his attempt to have Job abandon the God who had boasted about him, the God he served and loved. God restored Job's body. He healed his mind and gave Job more than he had before the trials began. He gave Job several more children and more servants. Before the calamities struck he was rich in possessions and had influence in the territory where he lived, and after the trials he was even richer and more renowned, so much so that we recall Job even today.

God will boast of you if you are a true believer and worshiper, so amid all of your trials, remember Job's story because in his struggles Job reaffirmed God's love for him to Satan, who was putting him to the test. Job blurted out these words to his friends, who tried to comfort him but sometimes questioned why he was being put through such tribulations. "Surely you must be hiding some secret deeds that are causing such havoc in your life," they said. But Job was steadfast in his faith and told them, "Though he slay me, yet will I hope in him; I will surely defend my ways to his face. Indeed, this will turn out for my deliverance, for no godless man would dare come before him!" (Job 12:15–16). If God did not give Job, a true believer, over completely to Satan to be lost forever to eternal damnation, why should He do this thing to you who are also believing and striving in His righteousness? He simply would not do this to you who love Him.

God told Satan that Job would not falter or cease to worship and praise Him despite what Satan would do. God boasted to Satan that Job was blameless and upright. Job had no desire or tolerance for evil. Can God say this same thing about you? Has He given you over to be tempted and tried because He believes that you will not crumble under the test? Did you know that God equips us with all that we need to survive and to rise above each test in our lives? His wish is that not one of us will be lost but that all of us will have a more abundant life.

Remember that it is through God that we will be victorious when facing these challenges. Maybe you have heard that patience is a great virtue. Here is another maxim to consider and remember: the race goes not to the swift but to those who can endure. Ecclesiastes 9:11 tells us that "the race is not to the swift or the battle to the strong, nor does food come to the wise, or wealth to the brilliant or favor to the learned; but time and chance happen to them all." Who is in charge of time and chance?

God in His own time frees us from each circumstance when we have endured enough to build courage, wisdom, and strength. Wisdom emanates from faith built by experiences with God in the vessel. When we have God in our vessels we smile at the storms of life. He steers the vessels of our lives more expertly than we can. When foul winds threaten to drive us into the rocks that lie hidden beneath the waters we sail, He skillfully guides us safely to home port.

Jesus Christ was the humblest man who ever walked this earth. He personified humility in all of His ways. Though He was strong, He did not operate out of His physical strength but out of His spiritual strength. He got angry but only because men defied God and defiled the things of His Father. Jesus exhibited a righteous anger. He used force in the temple, turning over the tables and dumping an assortment of things that were being used to commit robbery and other sin in His Father's name. He knotted a rope and drove out the thieves corrupting the temple, but this was a righteous anger.

Jesus instructs us to get angry if need be but not to remain in anger. We must forgive those who incite us to anger by trespassing against us and not allow the sun to go down without trying to alleviate the anger we have harbored. How do we alleviate this anger? It is quite simple! If someone upsets or irritates you, confront the matter in an understanding way. Do not attempt to bring harm or discomfort by seeking retribution, but try to bring about peace. If you have brought discomfort or pain in someone's life, you must apologize or make restitution before the sun goes down on your missteps. Simple mistakes can fester and grow into mistrust and even hate. By your lack of action, you may bring someone to sin and damnation if the person retaliates in anger. That is why we see what we call senseless violence or senseless murders.

A multitude of Scripture verses deal with anger and where we may find ourselves if we yield to it. Many passages also tell us about the benefits of being slow to anger, a mindset that demonstrates wisdom. If you are a person who constructs mottos to remind yourself how to live, here is a nice one: "In my anger, I will not sin."

Strength in Passivity

Jesus was the premier example of humility, and to secure just rewards you must pattern yourself after Him. But how do you do this in a society that says you must always be number one and must constantly strive to maintain that position? To gain number-one status and to be satisfied with yourself, you have to know that you have left no casualties along the way. If you have maligned, cursed, stepped on, dehumanized, cheated, or disregarded anyone in achieving your goals, you are not number one. You are closer to a zero.

"That's the way the system works! And if you don't conform you get left behind." How many times have you heard this?

Do you wish to be conformed to the world? You can live in this world and not conform to its ways. One person can make a change! If one person and then another and still another work toward making a desired change, soon enough there will be a shift in the atmosphere. Society's norms are shaped by its people, and conformity to these norms is not always the best solution. Radical change can spring from humble beginnings, the movement growing with the realization that it will bring a much better life.

The movements of Martin Luther, Mahatma Gandhi, and Dr. Martin Luther King Jr. prove that passivity can bring results. They advanced radical ideas through passive resistance. We can slay giants and move mountains this way. In contrast, violence brings devastation and death rather than brotherly love. But what if those pursuing passivity suffer violent deaths?

To the kingdom way of thinking, such a death is beautiful. That is beyond the understanding of those conformed to the world. The world deems the destruction of the passive one a success, but such success condemns the destroyer to the pit of fire for eternity. This false success, however, has insured a new life in the kingdom of heaven for the passive victim. Although destroyed in the flesh, the victim will rise in the spirit.

When we read or hear the Word, we ought to focus on gaining knowledge and to set aside the temptation to debate or challenge every sentence. We must receive the information in totality before forming an opinion. When we apply these restraints, we will gain new insights and knowledge about the kingdom of God. In life, resistance is sometimes necessary, but how about passive resistance? It has been shown to be effective.

Some critics will say, "Nice guys finish last," and they could never accept passivity. But passivity does not mean that we must deny ourselves everything in life. Passivity is consistent with sound lifestyle—obeying our parents, going to school and applying ourselves to the best of our ability, observing the laws of the land, studying the Word of God and living by it. An attitude of passivity is not a great leap from what we already know and practice. Being a nice guy is not a bad thing, but we need to be more than that.

God is always standing by ready to carry us whenever we are weary in body or in mind. All we have to do is maintain a welcoming heart and spirit based in faith and knowledge, and He will give us the ability to live victoriously. Let us rejoin Moses as God showed him his error in believing that he was insufficient even with divine help.

Think how God must have felt when He recalled how He had chosen the spirit of Moses to be placed in the womb of his mother

Jochebed. God had carefully and wonderfully crafted all the details. Moses was raised in the house of Pharaoh and schooled under the finest of tutelage in Egypt. God would complete His servant's training over a forty-year period while Moses lived as a shepherd in Midian. After all this, Moses came before God and told Him he did not feel up to the task of returning to Egypt to free the Israelites.

God was angry but patient. He invested Moses with even more power, allowing him to lift up his staff to command miracles in the Lord's name. God was merciful. He saved Moses's life at the inn after the prophet's prolonged and deliberate procrastination. If we follow the exploits of Moses, we will see that he became one of the greatest leaders in the Bible. He learned how to make good decisions, to manage, to delegate, to negotiate, and to communicate at an amazing level. Moses, who had a problem with stammering, became a gifted speaker. His last words, remembered as the Song of Moses, are forever etched in the history of God's people.

Detractors may say that Moses was a failed leader because he was driven to anger by the people he led. His anger was such that as punishment God denied him his final goal, reaching the Promised Land. I disagree with that argument. At the end of Moses's life, the Lord took him to the top of Mount Nebo. Before Moses was laid to rest there, God showed him every square inch of the Promised Land that He had promised His people beginning with Abram.

Moses died a physical death, but his spirit was transported to heaven where he dwells with God and the angels. His true rewards were in heaven, not in the Promised Land. And when Jesus Christ stood on the mount of transfiguration, seeking reassurance and motivation, Moses came down from heaven and was there by Jesus's side.

My Testimony of God's Promise

I can testify that the hand of God has worked in my life. When I was a small boy, others recognized that my dreams were eventful and full of meaning, so much so that a friend and associate of my grandfather would often ask what I had dreamed and try to interpret those dreams. That person told me at an early age that I would travel across the seas to America where I would be successful but would face great hardships and be married four times. That prophecy came true.

I often said, "Lord, I have done what You have asked me to do. Why then did You allow this to happen to me?" In 2006, after much listening, I heard God answer, "So that you may have a testimony in your mouth, but know that I am your God and that I will heal you."

I suffer from hereditary polycystic kidney disease. In 2005 both of my kidneys failed as I was working to spread the Word of God and to help build a house of worship to accommodate God's people. I wondered why God couldn't have prevented my kidney failure. Many of you have encountered issues and may be facing them even as you share my story. My experience shows that God is present in all of our struggles. He deflects some troubles so that we don't experience them but allows others to strengthen our faith.

Before this happened, God asked that I leave my long-established location in the Northeast United States and move to Florida. In 2002 I resigned my position, sorted out my business, said my good-byes, and moved. He told me to say yes to someone who had been asking me to relocate and to begin a relationship, and I agreed about six months before moving. I had been saying no for a long while, but God used this situation to prod me out of the Northeast, even though I had reservations about doing this. I went to south Florida and tried to make the best of the situation, but this was not meant to be a long-term relationship. It was just the means to bring me close to where God wanted me to settle permanently.

Naturally in such situations, feelings get hurt based on wishes and expectations, but when God leads, every situation adds to His glory. At the beginning of 2003 I moved from south Florida to central Florida. I had started a new career in mortgage financing while in south Florida. Continuing in my position as a mortgage consultant, I now had to drive an hour and a half to and from my office on highway I-95 each day. The long hours of commuting would serve a purpose in the journey God intended for me. I would use the knowledge I gained to help build a house of worship. This project was the reason God had me to move from the Northeast.

Shortly after relocating to central Florida, I had a dream in which I was approached by a black man who was six feet to six feet five and weighed 250 to 270 pounds. His color was dark but ashen and dull as if he were dead, and he had no signs of natural oils in his skin. He immediately attacked me. I punched him several times in defense, but my blows had little effect on him since I'm less than 150 pounds and just over five feet six. He grabbed me, threw me to the ground, and jumped on top of me. He kept me flat on my back while he pounded his belly on mine. I could not throw him off of me until he was finished doing what he intended to do.

When I thought about the dream the next day, I said to myself, *Lord, I don't understand what that was all about, but I hope it was not a homosexual attack.* I could not imagine what else it might have been since the man was assaulting me in a manner that appeared sexual. I had no such desires and prayed for God's protection from whatever might take place. I had once before had an experience with this spirit, and my finances were a shambles for many years after that. In the dream, this same man met me in a store where I had bought a lottery ticket. He grabbed the ticket out of my hand, and all of my efforts to get it back failed. Not one person dared to help me, but God helped me throughout my financial struggles. He saved me many times from total financial collapse.

My second encounter with this spirit had taken place on a weekend. Monday morning I took my usual hour-and-a-half drive south on I-95 to the office. I arrived just before nine o'clock, proceeded to my desk, and began to work. Shortly after, I began to feel woozy and nauseated. I tried to ignore the symptoms, but they worsened. I told my team manager I was not feeling well and needed to go to the hospital. He told me to alert the HR manager. She asked me if I knew how to get to the hospital, and I replied no. She told me she was about to run an errand and would drop me off there. I agreed.

I quickly went through the triage process; my vitals were taken, blood was drawn and an EKG ordered, and then a CAT scan. I was given an IV bag and medicine, and then I think I passed out. When I awoke I was being told about the seriousness of my condition. My kidneys were shutting down, and tests showed only a 25 percent function remaining. I was advised of the treatment options available to me and the best course of action given my condition and my family history. I certainly was not ready to hear all of this, but I did not forget to pray.

While this was taking place, a cousin in the Northeast was on the telephone speaking to her aunt, another cousin of mine. In the midst of their conversation the Spirit of God broke in and told my younger cousin, "You need to pray right now for Nathan. He is under attack." She told her aunt that the conversation had to stop. They are both women of faith, and they began to pray hard for me.

My cousin told me later that she called my dad after praying and asked him about me, but all he knew was that I had left the house and had gone to my job much earlier in the day. She told him to have me call her, and then she reached out to my friend and pastor in the Northeast, who called another friend and church brother. We later hooked up in a three-way call to my hospital room, and they prayed fervently that I would win my fight.

I remained in the ICU until the evening when doctors were sure that I had been stabilized. I was placed in a private room. Soon after, I called my dad, told him what had transpired, and gave him the contact information for the hospital, asking that he share it only with people close to me. I soon began to receive calls and prayers. My cousin later told me that when she began praying for me, she was shown a picture of me walking in a forest. Every leaf, every limb, every trunk, every shrub, every blade of grass was a scorched dry, and I was alone. She began to cry and to beg for mercy, and I am here to tell you this story today. The Lord God had mercy on me and saved me from that first demonic attack on my kidneys.

God knows whom to commission to help us fight our battles in the physical world. For the most part, physical troubles emanate from the realm of darkness, and so He sends the spiritually equipped. Those He sent me knew the language of heaven and shined their lights into the dark places. Their heavenly tongues beat back the man of ashes who attacked and dared to try to bring destruction upon me. The church brother of my pastor friend in the Northeast has a baritone voice that thunders when raised, and he raised his voice to the heavens that evening. That was the first time I had heard his voice, and the telephone could not contain it during that prayer session.

Later that night when I had gone to sleep, I dreamed that my mother, who had passed on a little more than ten years earlier, appeared in my room and sat on my bed. She spoke to me lovingly and looked as she did in life, but something in my spirit told me to be careful about accepting her. She said she wanted me to come with her, but I refused to go. She became very angry with me and said in a demanding voice, "The next time I appear, you'd better come." She left and I woke up, knowing that the Devil had tried to trick me by using my mother's image. I did not fall for this ruse, for she never before spoke to me in that demanding tone. I quickly recuperated in the hospital and was strong enough to leave Saturday afternoon.

In 1989 a friend told me that in a vision he had seen me in a Southern state, perhaps Georgia or Florida, and that I was getting married to a woman with children. In 1992 or 1993, another dear evangelist friend told me that God would use me to help build a church and a ministry in Florida. A few years later she told me that God was preparing a wife for me but that this woman was not yet in Florida. She would be coming from the Northeast, and God was fixing a situation in her life. She had to be freed from a difficult relationship. I did not dwell on this information because I was not ready for all of this to happen. I was rebuilding my own life at that time.

After I left the hospital in January of 2003, I lived in my father's home temporarily. I wanted to regroup financially and to return to south Florida to try the single life again. But God's plans were already underway and superseded mine. They were mightier than I realized. God is always right alongside of us in whatever we do or endure. I now recognize that this has been true throughout my life.

I had attended a Baptist church in south Florida, but now it was too far away. To get to that church, I would have to add another three quarters of an hour to the hour and a half I was driving to work. So I began attending my dad's church, which was not of the same denomination. The praise and worship were great, and so were the preaching and the Sunday school, but something was missing. I needed another church.

I often traveled on a certain route and saw many churches along the way. I decided I would visit them and see what they were like. One was of the Baptist denomination and the others were of unknown affiliation. After three months of worship at my dad's church, I visited one of these churches. It was in a strip mall and not in a traditional building with a steeple. I was greeted at the door by a young man whom I later got to know as a prophet and a preacher. "Are you a pastor?" he asked. "No, I am just a visitor," I replied. He seemed baffled but ushered me into the sanctuary where I was seated.

I never visited the other churches until many years later, because I had followed the Spirit of God to the right place. That was the church where the Lord God wanted me to help with the building. He had also positioned my new wife there. She had moved from the Northeast and had been baptized in that church.

We got married in a small private wedding at the church. Finances were limited. She was working two jobs, and my company had gone belly up during the mortgage industry crisis. The company was competing with the big boys in the marketplace in thirty states and got hammered by the improper practices that brought the industry to its knees. The firm abandoned prime customers. They were the better choice as I saw it, but those who owned and ran the business had other ideas. They wanted to chase after the subprime market, and this strategy was eventually fatal.

My wife and I rented a house and began life with some of her children in the home. We share many children; they are now adults except for our last, who is in college. The Lord God presented the youngest to me in a vision four years before her conception, and five years after that vision she was born. She is beautiful and vibrant and has a heart for God. She was led by the Spirit of God to show her faith in the work I was doing to help build the church. During a fundraising campaign, she pledged her spending money to the project.

At age ten she willingly planted a seed that will give great yield in God's kingdom. She purchased materials to help complete the church. To some this might not seem like much, but when a child is not being compelled to do something for God and steps forward to give up her spending money, that is monumental.

I love all of my children whether they are biological or inherited through marriage. I treat them all as lovingly as I can, and this has not been easy. I have had to be stern with some of them at times and to show more patience with others, always trying to steer them in the right direction. My children have disappointed and frustrated me, loved and cared for me, and left me pleasantly surprised and proud of them. These are the ups and downs that we experience in life's journey. God knows how to challenge us to expand our horizons. I have the feeling that He has boasted about me many times.

Soon after I began attending this church, I realized that it was facing a financial challenge in its building program. The church had purchased a large plot of land and needed a financial structure that showed fiscal responsibility and future financial capability. It needed to make sound projections based on attendance, giving habits, and receipts to convince financial institutions to fund the building project. My knowledge and expertise helped.

The work intensified and my involvement stretched into many areas of ministry—so much so that I found my responsibilities at the church taking an increasing share of my time. I was the church administrator and held almost every other position you can think of except for pastor or bishop. I even headed the cleaning crew that descended on the church every week.

Not too long after making a commitment to help, I got a job at a new mortgage company. However, I quit after a few months of working on commissions alone. I had to pursue leads, and all the ones I got were terrible since no one I contacted qualified for loans offered by the company. The guidelines were too restrictive. I wrote many good mortgage loan applications within a short time, and the other loan officers were surprised at how good I was at cold calling and prospecting. When I told them I was leaving, they were eager to get my case files, hoping to see if any of the factors that had prohibited those clients from getting loans had changed. I never followed up to see how many loans materialized, but I would not have received commissions since I had left the company.

Based on my résumé I was hired as a supervisor at a customer service call center, but three months into a four-month work contract, hurricanes devastated the area. That central Florida project was canceled and the work outsourced elsewhere. In 2005 I got a job as a distribution manager, but it did not live up to its billing as a management-level position. Working with independent contractors has its downside. If they don't show up, and you have a product that must go out at a certain time or become unusable, then you as the manager wind up delivering it to avoid ending up in the loss column. In addition, you don't want to wind up with a tarnished reputation as a manager. The company was great, but the job did not suit my education and training, and most of all the pay did not equal the sacrifices I had to make.

Two weeks before the ninety-day probationary period ended, I tendered my resignation. I knew long before then that I would quit. My wife was telling me to resign, but since she alone would be working, I wanted to get a few more paychecks to help with our needs. I had told only my wife what I was about to do, but three days before I quit, the young prophet in the ministry foretold what would happen. He prophesied that someone would have to give up his job, because that person had been working when God did not want him to do this. God would provide for the person's needs.

Sometimes it is better to be silent even when the prophecy fits you. Since I was not called to stand and to receive the word or to confirm to the prophet that he was hearing from God, I saw no reason to jump up and let everyone know what was going on in my life. I did not confirm or deny the prophecy, but I left the job three days later. The Lord God had brought me to that ministry from more than a thousand miles away to build the new church, and my focus was not to be on fixing my personal finances.

Many years before I arrived, someone prophesied that God was sending a man from the Northeast who could help the ministry to build and that he would marry a lady from the congregation. He would be successful and financially capable and would bring stability to her life. My wife is of different origin from mine. I am Jamaican American, and she was the one whom God was preparing for me. God had enabled her to escape her situation in the Northeast. When she came to central Florida she began to work but then sickness struck. She recuperated from her illness and went back to work. Thank God that she is still doing well.

When I arrived in central Florida in 2003, I was just getting by. My attempt to rebuild a career in the Northeast was cut short, and I had to start over in Florida. My liquid assets were used up, and I was subsisting on a paycheck that never seemed to be enough. God allowed me to remain in a state of dependence and humility. During my adult life, I had always been the chief breadwinner and had never been in a situation where my partner or my wife had that role. Now I had to accept my new role because I was reminded that God did not want me to work. He wanted to take care of my needs in a way I did not yet understand.

In 2004 I declared chapter-seven bankruptcy and wiped out my debts except for my student loans. They were growing exponentially, and I had no way to pay them. Each deferment brought on more interest and financial uncertainty. In the last month before quitting my manager's position in September 2005, I began to experience nausea and pains in my abdomen. I was no longer taking blood pressure medications, because I had no medical coverage. I was trusting that God would keep me from all issues. I had suspected a decline in my kidney function because the Spirit of God always alerts me to unusual negative spiritual activity and I had been experiencing just that. My wife wanted me to visit the emergency room at a local hospital, but I held out for several weeks until I could no longer do so. I could not keep food down when I ate, but I did not want to accept kidney dialysis as a way of life. I had seen my mother go through dialysis for nine years before she passed away, and I did not want this treatment. I was in denial about my kidney failure and did not own up to it until the evening I had to enter the hospital.

I had to go because the pain was excruciating and the nausea was too much. I was immediately admitted after undergoing routine tests and was informed that if I did not give my permission for dialysis I would soon die because my kidneys had shut down. I was lucky that I had not delayed any further. In October 2005 as my wife stood with me, we made the decision to go ahead with the required treatment plan. I had to be operated on to have a device implanted in my belly. An extended tube would protrude from my belly button, and I would receive peritoneal dialysis there in the future. I needed another surgery to my shoulder and neck area to establish a connection to my main artery for immediate dialysis procedures.

There were complications to the surgery plans because I had a huge hernia in the area of my stomach where doctors needed to install the device. The hernia was removed, and during my three years on dialysis I had several other hernias repaired. On my first night in the hospital, I was placed in the intensive care unit and was in an unresponsive condition for a long time. Vigilant and prayerful, my wife remained by my side, and church members, friends, and associates offered many prayers. They knew I was fighting for my life. Family called friends, and friends called other friends as well as pastors, asking their congregation to pray. My pastor offered prayers and asked others to pray. My dear pastor friend in the Northeast asked her congregation and friends to pray. She also kept up direct communications with my former pastor in central Florida and remained in contact with my wife and my family.

On my thirteenth day in the ICU, my wife, my pastor, and my father were gathered with my doctors in my room and were told to expect the worst because doctors had done everything they knew and my condition had not improved. I could hear the conversation but was unable to respond. I can't say whether I heard the conversation in a normal physical manner or through the spirit, but I heard it.

But something happened on the morning of the fourteenth day. God worked a miracle in His perfect way. The number fourteen is a doubling of God's perfect number seven, and on that day I received a double portion of His blessings. I sat up in my bed early in the morning, and when visitors arrived they were amazed at the sudden turnaround. My wife, my family, my friends, my pastor, and my doctors were overjoyed. My nephrologist, who was appointed as the lead doctor on the first night, has told me and others many times that I was almost dead and that he saved my life.

God uses doctors, but He is the ultimate restorer of lives. That first doctor is no longer my nephrologist, but I was given a choice between two other doctors in the practice, and I chose one who is still my nephrologist and who has done a marvelous job of caring for me. On that first night in the hospital, I was also assigned an internist who later became my primary care doctor and still is. I note all this to show that God has always found great care for me. He continues to do that today.

I remained in the ICU another seven days before I was discharged. Many medical issues still had to be addressed, and I had to regain strength. I had been losing weight because I had not been able to hold much food in my system before entering the hospital, and after being admitted, I lost an additional nineteen pounds because I was on intravenous drip. I was now down to 119 pounds with a large, distended stomach. Previously I had hovered between 145 and 149 pounds.

Immediately after leaving the hospital, I had to undergo dialysis three days a week, with each session lasting four hours. Later that was reduced to three hours and forty-five minutes, and after toxins in my blood decreased, to three-and–a-half hours. Though I had been prepared for peritoneal dialysis, I could not start that method until about a year after beginning hemodialysis.

During this process I asked the Lord God why He didn't save me from all of this suffering. Dialysis was not an easy thing for me. There was much pain and discomfort. I had always been squeamish about needles, and those needles hurt. I still vomited after meals and suffered from nausea quite a bit. Acid reflux was my constant companion, and I had no strength. I had lost almost all of my muscle mass, and my bones were going as well. My teeth were disintegrating slowly but surely. I had worked so diligently to save my teeth, not to mention the cost of upkeep over the years. If you knew me before all of this took place, your first sight of me during this period would have left you aghast and thinking that I looked terrible.

I was determined not to be defeated. I never said no to any request made of me. The only way I would not come through for someone was if I was hospitalized, and I was hospitalized repeatedly. There were several hospitals within a ten-mile radius of my home, and I spent time in all of them for tests, for treatment, and for many surgeries. In a three-year period, I had thirteen surgeries. The last was a kidney transplant. So it should be clear why I asked God why He allowed me to endure all this suffering. I will repeat His answer to my bold question. God said, "So that you may have a testimony in your mouth, but know that I am your God and that I will heal you."

I had peritonitis, several hernia repairs, thyroid surgery, parathyroid surgery, surgeries to install catheters, surgeries to construct veins, and to top it all off, kidney transplant surgery. One rejection of the organ was warded off with early detection, a forceful plan of prevention and prayer, and God's guiding hand on my doctors and caregivers. I have had only one surgery since then—an emergency appendectomy. Since 2005 I have had fourteen surgeries, and I won't count the dental extractions. Each of those surgeries had to be carefully timed, planned, and executed. I had to be on antibiotics before, during, and after surgery. Infections are a no-no for me in my condition. I have lost much of the bone structure in my mouth and cannot have implants because there isn't enough bone to sustain them. Besides, that would be another foreign object that my body would seek to reject.

As a man, I rejected even the thought of certain procedures being done on me. I will mention two to emphasize that sometimes we may have to climb mountains we would avoid if given the choice. For a man, prostrate screening is intimidating, and shrinking the prostate gland the old-fashioned way is even more frightening. I had to endure the heat treatment process, and it seemed to take forever. Google the treatment process for yourself. But here is the other procedure that men fear. Simply to hear that someone wants to shove a tube up your penis is enough to make you run for the door or to crash through a window. Is that too dramatic? Okay, I'll rephrase. We would cringe and ask that some other means be explored and suggest that maybe the required test or procedure be canceled. No, doctor, we don't need that. We'll be all right without it.

But eventually I learned to endure the thing that made me cringe when I heard about it. With each occasion I became more fearless and accommodating in having it done. Sickness can cause you to surrender yourself to capable hands but only when you have entrusted yourself to God in the belief that Jesus Christ died on the cross for you. The knowledge that He suffered so that you would not have to suffer what He did gives you hope, and in that hope is redemption.

One time I had been prepped for major surgery. I had been given anesthesia and had said good-bye to my wife and was being wheeled into the surgical theater with the nurses standing over me.

That was the last thing I remembered. When I woke up in the recovery room, one of the nurses who had wheeled me in was there to check on me. When I was fully recovered, she asked, "What was that song you were singing?" I had no idea, but I know that it had to be a church song. I asked if she remembered the words, but she did not. Before I was put to sleep, I always prayed and encouraged myself with the knowledge that God is always there. I have been singing hymns, mostly gospel and worship songs, for many years, but I still do not know which song I was singing on that occasion.

On that October day in 2005 when I accepted that I had kidney failure, I allowed myself to be tested in a manner that would take me to the gates of death. I have spoken about this only once when the Spirit of God inspired me to mention the topic during a sermon to my church congregation in 2014. On a visit to the church, the prophetess who had said that I would be sent from the Northeast told me that I had been at the gates of death, but I did not discuss my experience. I just nodded my head because she was seeking acknowledgment that I was listening to her and that she was not lying. She enlarged upon the event, saying that the Devil thought he had me that time but that God let him know he could not take me because the Lord had His hands on me. I was His child and He had a mighty work for me to do.

During my twenty-one days in the ICU, there was a building boom in Florida. You could always spot a house being built. The streets were bustling with large trucks carrying pine logs that had been cut down and removed from building sites. Trucks were also hauling precut roofs and other building materials. Dump trucks were hauling sand and dirt for building sites. At these sites, mounds of freshly emptied dirt and sand waited their turns to be spread out and compacted into foundations and lawns. Because I had been unresponsive for so long and near death, when I was released from the hospital I experienced a desire I never had before.

Every time I saw those freshly poured mounds of sand and dirt, I had a great urge to stop the car and bathe in them or to scoop up handfuls and throw them all over myself. A strange sense of belonging kept pulling me toward the mounds. I was always conscious of these feelings and was careful not to act upon them or even to tell anyone about them. I had been so close to death that I craved the thing that covers the corpse: dirt. After several months of fending off these feelings with constant prayer, they went away.

Why I Was Unconquerable

I promised to explain why the Devil could not take me or trick me into accepting a partnership with him. From the beginning, I faced hardships but I thank God that my maternal grandparents Cathy and Ben were there to love me and to raise me in a Christian way while my mother worked in Kingston, Jamaica. My grandmother had hypertension, and when I was almost eleven, she had a stroke from which she never recovered. My grandparents were raising my older brother and me along with my grandfather's only son. My grandfather became quite ill sometime later, and my mom came home to be with us.

After we had exhausted all available medical options, my grandfather's family asked him to return to the village where he was born. His remaining brothers and sisters wanted to care for him in his last days. My mother was a child from my grandmother's previous union. My mother and I inherited the trait of hypertension from my grandmother, as did a few of my siblings.

I had no relationship with my biological father or with his side of the family until I was about eight years old. Families fall out over race, color, age, class, status, and many other issues. In our case it was about age and color. My mom was dark-skinned and my dad light-skinned, and she was nine years older than he was, so age was a problem as well. When I was forty-one or forty-two, my mom told me that before I was born my paternal grandmother said that I couldn't be her son's child because her son would not be involved with an old woman like my mother. He was seventeen and she was twenty-six. He was a boarder in Cathy and Ben's home; my mother had returned after a broken relationship, and the rest is history. When a woman's heart is broken and a handsome young man says he will help fix it, she sometimes throws caution to the wind. Even if it was a factor before, age no longer mattered in my father and mother's case.

My mother's parents were Christians and they raised us in the faith. They were members of a Baptist church and I was baptized there. They were not discriminatory Christians. We attended our Baptist church on Sunday morning, returning home by early afternoon. After dinner we would relax for a while and then attend the Church of God or a Pentecostal ministry in the evening. On Sundays we could not listen to dance music on the radio, and as kids we could not be caught singing songs considered improper or non-Christian or dancing on the Sabbath. We could not play sports such as soccer or cricket or any other games. We were to be found reading or sitting in silence. We did not mind going to church in the evenings because evening services were a spectacle for us children.

These services were dominated by singing often accompanied by shouting, dancing, and falling down in the Spirit. We always enjoyed ourselves, but when we were old enough to go on our own we wanted to sit in the rear of the church to giggle, to point, and to talk with friends during the services, which went on and on. Whenever we got caught someone would move us toward the front and promise to tell our grandparents that we were playing the fool in church.

My grandfather was originally from the same village and district that my father and his mother were from, and that is how arrangements were made for my dad to live with my mother's parents as a boarder. My mom's stepfather had relocated to a historic town prominent for its part in the slave revolt against the landowners and the British. That revolt was connected to other events leading to the abolition of slavery in Jamaica. The town had become a commercial center with businesses, schools, churches, the courthouse, and a jail. All major transportation came to that hub and fanned out in other destinations. My dad had come to be schooled as an apprentice in a suitable trade.

After the union that produced me, my father's mom and my mom's family had a falling out, and my dad had to pack up and leave. He stayed home until another arrangement was made for him to get his apprenticeship in Kingston. When I grew old enough to travel, I would accompany my grandfather Ben when he visited his family in the same district where my father's mom lived. After seeing me over a period of years, people began to ask my grandfather whose boy I was. Some who knew my dad and his family also knew that he had lived with my grandfather for a while, and they would comment that I looked just like my father, just darker. Those conversations made their way to my father's mom, and when she saw me things began to change.

My mom had suffered the loss of her mom, and taking care of my grandfather Ben and us became difficult. As a single mother and her father's caregiver, she found it hard to make ends meet. Jobs were scarce in our area, and that's why she had earlier lived and worked in Kingston. Luckily her parents had planned for their future after their marriage and had invested in property in an area that had opened up for purchase and settlement.

This prime property encompassed several acres and stretched all the way to the beach. The land was quite fruitful, and my grandfather built a home there and began farming. We had vegetables, coffee, cocoa, coconuts, bananas, breadfruits, avocados, mangoes, sugarcane, and tubers like yams. My grandfather also raised pigs and chickens, and there were fish in a pond formed from rainwater. The Atlantic Ocean was at the edge of our property. We had many things to consume and to sell to keep us going.

Keep going we did, but medical bills, transportation, school clothes, shoes, books, and other food items were expensive. My mother needed help! She contacted my father and told him she could no longer stay afloat on her own. His mother, my grandmother, had now been convinced that I was his son, so around my eighth birthday, he rode up on a huge BSA Triumph motorcycle and I began spending some of my summers in Kingston. I also visited my paternal grandparents at their home. There I met my father's side of the family. These relatives all accepted me. They would say, "The older you get, the more you look like your father" and "You are the dead stamp of your father." This last statement is the kind Jamaicans make to emphasize the correctness of their assessment.

My father's parents were farmers on a small scale. They owned property and rented some, growing crops and marketing them. My great- grandparents were farmers as well, and so were their sons. My grandmother and my great-grandmother would come to Kingston on Friday nights, and my father would take me to the market to visit. There I would also see my great-aunt, my aunt, and my uncle as well as my cousins. The men usually remained in the district, and after preparing the produce, the women would travel to the market to sell it. Nestled among the items for sale were special packages for relatives who lived in Kingston. People would come to pick up their packages and would greet relatives and get news of family and friends back in the district.

I was an observer during my first summer with my father, but I understood more fully the workings of this family after I had visited the district and stayed a while with my grandparents and the rest of my dad's relatives. That first summer I learned that my paternal grandparents were Christians. Farmers wake up early in the morning, but Christian farmers wake up even earlier to pray. At least that's how it appeared to me at the time.

My grandparents were raising three children belonging to my aunt, who was living in Kingston, and they added me in the summer. Everybody was up early, stretching, yawning, and bleary-eyed.

We gathered in my grandparents' bedroom for Scripture reading followed by prayers that seemed to go on for hours. We knelt down on the wooden floor throughout the ordeal. This was especially difficult for any child without pillows to cushion those tiny knees. We shifted from one knee to the next and hoped the prayers would end soon, but when we were called on to read or to pray, we knew we had to look like we were eager to participate. On Sundays we got dressed up and walked to the Church of God about three miles away. In church we could fan ourselves all we wanted, but there was no talking, no sleeping, and no playing. When we were good we were rewarded with a mint to suck on, but there was no chewing gum.

After spending a few summers with my dad and his family, I moved to Kingston to live with him. I had taken my common entrance exams and was ready to attend a school for older kids. I had outgrown primary school, but my experiences there were part of the reason the Devil could not hold on to me. I was a great student in primary school, and so one of my teachers began addressing me as Squire Palus. So much was expected of me in the next grade that when I fell short I regularly got my butt whipped by one teacher. A short, stocky woman with huge, flabby arms, she punished me with pleasure. Corporal punishment was the norm in school, and she often exercised this prerogative. She believed that if you answered a question incorrectly or not to her liking, word for word as she expected, you deserved a whipping.

She called on me quite liberally and used the squire title because she expected the best of her students. She had a huge leather belt and did not like the fact that I wore a new khaki uniform that had been introduced to the market. My dad bought several in Kingston when we went school shopping, and they were not yet common in the rural areas. When my mother washed, starched, and ironed them, they were stiff and held a sharp crease. Students sat at heavy wooden desks and could lean over them without toppling, so this teacher would come up behind a student, take him by the hand, lean him over the desk, and whack his butt for a while.

She did that to me and complained all the way about the khakis. She would pull my shirttail up from my pants to lessen the covering over my butt, and she would give me a few extra whacks. This teacher did not care who your father or mother was. The more important your parents were, the more she expected of you, and the same was true if you had a reputation as a good student. She would tell you that while she kicked your butt. Because I was a great student, I was expected to gain a full scholarship through the common entrance exams, which allowed students to attend the best secondary schools in the country. I was greatly disappointed because I took the exam twice and qualified for only a half scholarship each time, and they could not be combined to make a full scholarship.

My grandfather was building a house on our property when he died. It was a concrete structure with wood framing to section off rooms and with wooden floors. The veranda and the drawing rooms were rough cast but never got the tiles planned for them. The roof was part shingles on the upper portion covering the bedrooms and part zinc on the lower section covering the veranda or porch. Under the cedar flooring, the house had a partial crawl space. That section of the house sat on poured concrete posts about twenty-four inches high. As young kids we played under the house, and my grandparents and my mother sent us under the house to retrieve the eggs our chickens sometimes laid there. Our dog once had puppies under the house.

A quite distasteful history lay under the house. We would hear noises there at night and would assume dogs were to blame, but later we would find things that a dog would not bring there. At times we would hear dogs barking at night though no one was coming up the walkway. Our walkway was packed with broken stones and covered with gravel. We would hear the sound of someone walking on the gravel but would see no one there. Out of the blue things would fall on the roof, though we did not have a neighbor for at least two hundred yards.

We had neighbors on all sides as we were in the center of a tract of land that began on the eastern side of the main road. From that main road, a central public road extended all the way to the beach. On that road, on either side of our property two brothers held parcels of land that began at the top of that drive and extended about two hundred yards to our border line in the center. The land department had cut an easement in between those two parcels to make a private lane to our property. The two brothers and their families were okay with this arrangement when my grandparents first acquired the property, but after they saw what my grandparents did with it and how bountiful it was, they became quite sour. One of those families was more vindictive than the other.

One of the brothers and his family were known to practice witchcraft and bragged about how good they were at it, warning that people better not mess with them. They lived the closest to us and watched our every move. They threw garbage into our lane, let their animals roam there, and started arguments with us. They sometimes had religious ceremonies called *koumina* (pronounced *cumina*) by Jamaicans. These rituals have roots in African spirit worship, spirit bribing, and spiritual possession. Participants beat ceremonial drums, dance, and offer gifts to invite the spirits to possess them and to give them power and knowledge of whatever they are seeking. The spirits possess the dancers, some of whom are so affected that they go into trances. Some have to be tied up or sat upon to keep them from convulsing or running wild. I saw people running into the bushes at night after being possessed. I was curious as a child, but I kept my distance because I was afraid.

So what about the things under the house, small pen knives, little packages tied up in black tread, six-pence coins, scissors and broken dolls with straight pins, food offerings, and the sound of footsteps on gravel while the dogs barked, and the stuff falling on the roof of the house at night? We never got to see the actual stuff falling on the roof because we dared not venture outside of the house while these things were happening at nights. There were other notable phenomena, but I prefer to discuss my fight to pass the common entrance exam with a full scholarship. I had earned the title of squire because I was consistently number one in my class, and yet some of the dumbest kids passed and got full scholarships. Students were given two opportunities to take the test. The second time I took it, my grandmother was in the hospital, and I had an uneasy feeling that morning. As I sat in the classroom and began the test, I heard the bell at the Baptist church. I knew right away that my grandmother had passed. I did not get the official news until the first break in the testing when we could leave the classroom. Family acquaintances gave me the news. They were not taking the test and were not required to come in early, so they got the information regarding my grandmother early that morning.

I went to live in Kingston and attended a noted school there after the common entrance exams. My father had chosen a Methodist school that offered morning devotion, religion classes, and evening devotion before dismissal. At first, I did quite well because of my solid foundation, but after a while I went downhill. I was no longer the squire of old even with hours of study beyond the regular school day. I was just passing despite all my efforts.

I was now returning to my original parish during school breaks. My first time back, a son of one of the neighboring brothers challenged me to a fight in our lane. I was coming from the main road heading for our house, and he thought this was his opportunity to teach the former country boy now living in the city an unforgettable lesson. He did not know that I was studying judo under the tutelage of a professional instructor at my school and in my spare time exploring karate. Not only did I give him a pummeling, but I flipped him over my head into his family's barbed-wire fence along the lane. He went away with ripped clothes and ripped flesh. His father later came over to yell and to curse at my mother and threaten to get even. However, I know the encounter did not end there. I had been doing well in school before that fight, but thereafter my educational fortunes changed.

My father had married an American woman while I was spending summers in Kingston and hadn't yet moved there. She had been visiting Jamaica to spend time with my dad, living and working in America until it was time for him to migrate to the United States. A few years after they were married, their petition to the US Immigration and Naturalization Service was approved, and my dad was cleared to begin his new life in America. My dad soon traveled to America, and I was left in the care of a lady friend of his who lived with me in an apartment next door to my grand-aunt's apartment in the same house. About a year after, that lady got her approval to travel to America, so I went to live with my aunt, her husband, and their children. During that time, work was underway on my visa to travel to America to be with my dad, my stepmother, and my stepbrother.

After a few glitches I was ready to leave for America. My mother rented a passenger van to drive from her town to the airport with my grandmother and other relatives to see me off. The aunt whom I had been living with hired a car to take us to the airport, and we were all going to meet up there. However, the Devil struck. Thinking that I was going to ride in the passenger van with my mother and my grandmother, he caused them to have an accident. Another vehicle sideswiped their van, causing it to turn over. Praise God that they were praying people and were not seriously hurt. They just suffered cuts and bruises and the disappointment of being unable to meet us at the airport to see me off.

Nineteen years later, I met a man who brought that day back to my memory and pointed out that my neighbors where I grew up as a small boy thought I would be in that van. A way of escape was made for me. I was not in that van. I awaited a new life in America. Naturally I missed seeing my mother and my grandmother and everybody else who were coming to give me a proper sendoff. Still, I was happy that I had left certain people and things behind in Jamaica. And although I thought I had left the Devil behind for good, I soon found out that he had preceded me and was already living in America.

New in America

I landed in a major Northeastern city on a balmy night just before eight o'clock in November 1966. I was excited and full of anticipation. A stewardess escorted me from the plane, and I soon found myself in a tight embrace, caressed by two large arms and kissed lovingly. My father explained all of this by introducing me to my new step-grandmother. She was a wonderful lady, always caring and full of laughter. On top of that, she was a great cook who was always ready to feed me and to talk. We bonded immediately and shared that bond to the end.

We walked to a car driven by a family friend to make the journey home. My dad did not own a car at the time, and so his friend, who was a taxi driver, used his station wagon to transport us that night. I was wearing a tailored blue suit; in Jamaica it was not unusual to have suits and other garments tailored individually. Tailoring was a respected trade since everyone wanted to have smartly styled clothing in the tradition of the British colonists in Jamaica. My grandmother and I sat in the rear seat and talked about the flight, but I was eager to get my first look at the United States. I asked questions about everything I saw on the ride from the airport. My first impression was that America lacked color and was a dreary place.

We arrived at an apartment in a two-story private home in a suburb. The owner and her daughter lived upstairs, and we occupied the main-floor apartment. A welcome-home party was beginning. My stepmother was there along with her sister, a step-uncle, a few of my cousins, the taxi driver and his son, and a few friends of the family. My stepbrother was not there, and everyone in the family wondered what could be more important than showing up to greet me. However, he arrived later, and as the night wore on there was lots of music, dancing, eating, drinking, and fun. People had been anticipating that I would bring new Jamaican music not yet available in American stores, so soon after we had settled in, one of my cousins asked me to get those records so he could spin them on the turntable. He had been a notable performer on the dance hall scene in Jamaica. I had also brought Mr. J. Wray and his nephew along, so the party was now in full swing.

J. Wray and his nephew are special friends to many Jamaicans. Some recognize them as medicine men, others value their spiritual worth, and still others see them as the life of the party. Some Jamaicans declare that no home should be without a bottle of J. Wray and his nephew, otherwise known as Jamaican white rum. Someone in my home had become quite infatuated with Mr. J. Wray and his nephew.

I arrived on a Friday and the next day we went shopping and purchased a long corduroy overcoat with fleece lining. November in the Northeast United States can be quite balmy one day and quite cold the next. I got more acclimated to my surroundings on Sunday, and on Monday morning I was enrolled at a Catholic high school. My stepbrother was a student there in his sophomore year, and now I would attend this all-boys school. My dad had written me while still in Jamaica telling me how well my stepbrother was doing in school. He compared this with my declining performance and said it was time I did better. I was entering my freshman year.

Classes began early Tuesday morning. My first class was in math with a quiz covering the work students had done since September.

My teacher, a Franciscan brother, said he wanted me to take the test to assess where I was and what I might need to cover. I took the test and scored 100 percent. Little did I know that on that day I had raised jealousy in other students, in myhome, and would become a target.

My stepbrother rode the bus and the subway with me to and from school on Tuesday. We rode together Wednesday morning, and I waited for him in the afternoon after classes but could not find him, so I went home alone. My stepbrother arrived home later. He wanted to see if I could find my way home by myself. I don't remember if my stepmother had returned from work or had called from work to find that I had come home alone, but she was not pleased about how that had happened. She made it clear to my stepbrother that she was displeased with what he had done, but to me it was no big deal. I was determined to make my mark in this new arena regardless of the challenges I faced.

The next Saturday my stepbrother and I met up with a friend and visited a noted downtown shopping district. We took a subway ride that was dismal compared with my first week's experience. This was a different line and ran underground all the way. We caught a taxi to the subway and descended into the tunnel, with the smells of earth, metallic shavings, and moisture contending for recognition. More interesting than the décor were the people and their mannerisms. I noted the passengers entering and exiting the train in different sectors and could trace the city's social makeup in one subway ride.

My stepbrother and I had grown closer and had built a strong bond. Some of his friends would later comment, "If I see one of you, I know that the other is close by." On weekends we hung out with friends and went to parties and high school basketball games. Attending basketball games was fun. My stepbrother was a manager for our school's junior varsity team and was ecstatic when he received his team jacket because the team became division champion.

My stepbrother got a job at a supermarket chain. I was fifteen and needed to be sixteen to get working papers. My brother knew I wanted to work, because I often mentioned my desire to help my family in Jamaica. One day he came home and told me that he knew a way I could work unofficially at the store. I would not work inside the store, but I would help the guys who made grocery deliveries for tips. That was good enough for me. I spoke to my dad and my stepmother, and they said it was okay for me to do this. Thus began my work history in the United States.

The store delivered groceries with two vans. Each driver sometimes had a helper. Deliveries were for customers who didn't want to waste time and energy carrying groceries home. The store was located in an area with many affluent people, artists, actors, musicians, dancers, and writers. The normal van service had sometimes failed to provide the swift deliveries promised, so the store managers sometimes pulled stock workers from the aisles to make short runs with bicycles fitted with grocery carriers. Workers sometimes used shopping carts if the bicycles were already out. The busier it got the more groceries I delivered to apartments where I collected tips in change, dollar bills, and sometimes redeemable bottles that I cashed in at the store.

So where did the Devil come in, and how did I overcome him? Sometimes the Devil does not enter like a roaring lion but slips in gently like a lamb so as not to alert us to his presence. Nevertheless, he is lurking and making notations. He gives us the impression that we are home free, and some of us are fooled into letting go of or forgetting who has kept us safe. Even sadder, some make worthless idols their gods. Then Satan pounces on us like a savage lion because we have thrown away the protection of Christ Jesus.

The spring semester was over, grades were sent home, and now the comparisons began. I had done quite well and made the honor roll, but my stepbrother had slipped below his usual standard. At home questions were asked and comments made regarding his abilities and his need to buckle down and to focus. Summer was upon us and we were eager to work all season to fulfill our wish lists. We would buy leather jackets, knitted alpaca sweaters, silk slacks, alligator shoes, and maybe snakes if we could acquire enough money. We were going to be out of sight as we said in those days. Sharp was also acceptable in the vernacular of the hip crowd, and we would be clean and sharp and everything else that was good. My birthday arrived and I could now obtain my working papers. I had become well known and well liked from hanging out at the store and making deliveries. I was a nice Catholic school boy who was respectful and quiet. I had no trouble getting hired to work to do deliveries for the store on Friday evenings and Saturdays during the days. My stepbrother's satisfactory work record also helped me.

I made the best of my opportunity, and soon I was promoted to stock boy with occasional deliveries. My stepbrother had been trained and was promoted to front-end assistant where he did overrides and voiding of charges, checked cashiers in and out, and provided change for the registers. He was a six feet three, a handsome young man with presence, and the managers needed that presence in the front of the store. Shoppers had to check any bags they brought into the store, and my stepbrother helped with that security protocol.

The store was in a great location, but sometimes it was beset by undesirables. A private plainclothes security guard roamed the store, and I was surprised to see some of the people he caught shoplifting. They were often dressed in suits and fur coats, and most of us would not have identified them as thieves if we had not seen them in the act or caught them with merchandise that they did not pay for. My brother was up front to deter a rush at the cash register or the front office where the safe was kept. In 1967 marijuana and hashish were plentiful, but heroin was king. People were hooked and strung out all over the city, and they committed bold acts to make money to support their habits. Some shoplifters were hungry, but others came in to steal pricy steaks, legs of lamb, large roast beef cuts, and other items to peddle for money.

Still, we had gained jobs and unique experiences that were building our characters. My stepbrother was older than I, more connected, and more advanced as far as girls and the American culture. He was the teacher and I was the shy student who had not yet blended old ways with new, life- changing transformation. I was coming into my own slowly while he was moving at an accelerated pace. We went to parties in the summer and hung out with friends until it was time to return to school in the fall. We worked no more than the twenty hours a week that the law allowed at our age but managed to buy new clothes and new shoes. The school dress code called for a suit and a tie or a jacket, slacks, and a tie. Sneakers were allowed only in gym class. I did not care for them, so I had only a pair for gym.

The first marking period was okay for both of us, but thereafter my stepbrother struggled. He would work more hours than I, sometimes even on Sundays since he was being asked to cover for the assistant manager. Later on he would close the store at night since he had been there long enough to be trusted as capable and responsible. During his junior year, he met a girl with whom he was smitten. She lived in another city, but they were inseparable. She was a Catholic school girl and her mother was not too keen on her having a boyfriend, but eventually they married and had a child.

My stepbrother was spending a lot of time away from home with school, work, and a girlfriend, but during that time God revealed more clearly to me what was going on. I had seen signs of trouble earlier with my stepmother's constant nitpicking at me, her complaints to my father, and her tendency to make mountains out of molehills. I had caught a bad cold during my first spring in America. My stepmom took me to the doctor and complained about having to do this and about the three-dollar copay, the antibiotic prescription, and the cough medicine that was prescribed.

The next day when she asked me if I had taken the medicine, I told her that I had, but she kept badgering me about it, harping on the fact that the medicine had cost her money. My father was out somewhere, and when he came home she accosted him with a major complaint and lots of vitriol. The Devil reared his head, and my father took the complaint far too seriously. I cannot erase this memory. The landlady came downstairs and knocked at the door to ask if everything was okay. Assured that it was, she went back upstairs.

My father had acted toward me in a way he had never done before, and this told me that he had been fed an ever-growing stream of lies and exaggerations. Our relationships were strained but we went on. My stepbrother was spending almost every bit of free time with his girlfriend and was constantly talking to her on the telephone, and his grades were unacceptable. I tried my best to be respectful and diligent at home, at school, and at work, and the rewards were great. I was on the honor roll, and I was promoted to be a display person at the store. Previously, only full-time grocery clerks would construct the store displays, but the managers were pleased with my work, so they rewarded the likable Catholic high school boy with the responsibility and with the raise that came with it.

Each week management gives a display person a list of sale items that are to be promoted and stocked throughout the week. The employee then constructs displays at both ends of the aisles and at other strategic places in the store. He also hangs large sales signs in the front show windows and removes and replaces letters and numbers on the store's marquee outside. I was good at reading plans and diagrams. Though construction of the displays was sometimes quite demanding, especially when they entailed heavy items such as large canned goods, I was able to manage alone. Sometimes, though, I needed help lifting items to the top, even though I had built upper-body strength from handling hundreds of product-filled boxes.

Spending time at home, I observed more closely our family makeup. Many things were revealed in words and actions. The tongue is unruly as a serpent and can bring forth curses as well as blessings, and the prophet Jeremiah tell us that the heart of man is deceitful (Jeremiah 17:9).

I was naïve in the beginning and did not think there was anything wrong with my stepmom telling me, "Pick up the mail each evening when you get home from school, and do not allow it to remain in the mailbox until your father gets home from work." My dad found out the hard way what was happening when the sheriff came to his job to take charge of his paycheck. He told me this only a few years ago. I don't know whether he had withheld the story out of embarrassment or disappointment, but I was a child then and did not need to know. My stepbrother had called me one day to come into my parents' room while our mom was taking a bath in the locked bathroom. He had opened her pocketbook and in it was more than six hundred dollars in cash. However, before entering the bathroom she had told him she had no money to give to him.

Some people are all about living for now and having a great time. They will eat, drink, and be merry and will avoid doing anything for others. Self-absorption gets in the way of being a good shepherd. A parent may resist helping a child, fearing the child will grow up to accomplish more in life than she has done. Jesus Christ taught us quite the opposite. He said we shouldn't worry about tomorrow, because our Father in heaven will take care of our needs. He also said we ought to care for one another and not withhold what we have to give. We should not tell others to come back tomorrow when we have enough to share today.

The day after Thanksgiving my brother and I were relaxing in our room discussing the holiday when he made a comment I was not expecting. "Let's face it, man," he said. "Our mother is off the hook." This was a slang expression comparing someone to a telephone removed from the receiver so that callers get a busy signal. She had invited several people to our home for dinner and drinks, but they had other commitments. My stepbrother and I kept our eyes on one person who did attend, and although we didn't communicate during the gathering, it turned out we both came away with the same conclusion that this person had hidden benefits. My stepbrother then jumped up, got dressed, and said, "I'll see you later, man. I gotta get out of here." He did not return until seven hours later.

We moved to another apartment after a few years. Our first apartment, located in a quaint house, had two bedrooms. This one, located in another private home on a nearby street, had three. My brother and I held a memorable hooky party before we moved. He planned it and then told me about it. I had no knowledge of such things but I learned fast. We were not skipping school, because the party was planned for a Catholic school holiday when public schools had classes. The public school students who attended were the ones skipping school. The other teenagers brought beer, liquor, and smokes, and we provided the house and the music.

My dad left for work first, and shortly after my stepmom left the house the telephone began to ring off the hook. Contacts were calling to see if the coast was clear. We also had to be sure the landlady and her daughter were out of the house. We waited until we saw them leave before telling friends to come over. The partygoers streamed in, and because the word got out far and wide, there were teenagers in our apartment, in the hallways, and on the stairway leading up to the landlady's apartment. I made a mistake and did not eat before the crowd gathered. When I had a rum and coke, I felt woozy, so I got in my bed and fell asleep.

Later some girl woke me up, asking me if I had seen her private parts. She was sitting on my bed, but I was too buzzed to respond and went back to sleep. I got up later and brushed my teeth. Someone who did not know me kept knocking on the door, so with toothbrush in hand and toothpaste in my mouth, I opened the door to see what was so urgent. He told my brother, "Hey, there is some guy in your bathroom brushing his teeth with your toothbrush." When my brother saw me, he told the dude, "Hey, that guy is my brother," and we all laughed uncontrollably.

As the party continued, somebody caused another person to fall over a coffee table, and one of the legs got broken. A young lady drank too much and passed out. Someone put her on my parents' bed, and when it was time to end the party before any adults returned she was still knocked out. A group of guys had her arms slung over their shoulders and were walking her out to a car rubber legs and all when the landlady arrived. The outside garbage cans were full of beer and liquor bottles and cigarette butts, and no one had time to dispose of the messy evidence. Our main boys stayed to help us clean up the apartment and to set the table on its feet so that everything looked perfect, but the landlady saw the bottles and the guys carrying the girl out of the house, and just like that, we were busted. Sounds like a movie script, but this was real!

We were severely reprimanded by the adults, and I was considered a terrible disappointment. I did not plan the party, but my stepbrother and I had built a bond, so I did not throw him under the bus, and he did not blame me either. All they could get from me was, "I don't know anything." However, a few weeks after the party, on a Saturday afternoon when I was cleaning and polishing the coffee table, the hitched-up broken leg came off, and there was nothing I could do to fix it. So much for dutifully doing my weekend chores! I had no explanation for why the leg was broken, but the adults figured out that the party was to blame, and I was on the passenger list for a flight back to Jamaica.

New Friends in Fulfillment

Summer was approaching and the weather was good. I had not been working many hours in the evenings after school, because I wanted to study for final exams. I would see several young people passing my house as they walked a dog and then turning onto the main road to go to their homes. Usually there were two or three girls, one of them Hispanic, and two black girls with two or three black boys. The girls were beautiful and the boys seemed friendly, so I decided to introduce myself. We became friends, and it turned out they all lived on the same block just down the street. I kept visiting and wound up meeting their parents. Two of these people played roles in my life thereafter.

One boy was named Shing, and his mother had recently purchased a two-family brick house and needed a tenant for the top floor, which had three bedrooms. I told my parents, they investigated and worked out the details, and we relocated to the second floor in Shing's home. The second key person was the older of the two black girls, who became my girlfriend, my fiancée, and then my wife and the mother of my oldest child. A third person on that street also became instrumental in my future, but he was not one of the teenagers I met; he was an adult. Before I go any further, I must take a step back to my early days in America when we were still living in the first apartment.

I loved to watch all kinds of programs on television, but I preferred one channel over all the others. One event would change the lives of billions of people, and I watched it on that channel with a certain newsman narrating the story. On July 20, 1969, three American astronauts spearheaded man's first landing on the moon, and the coverage was nail-biting to say the least. But beyond this, the Lord reached down that day and anointed me to be involved with broadcast television and with that newsman. I wanted to see the studios, the newsman, and the mock-up of the moon's surface they had used. And all this happened later as God ordained it on that day.

I enjoyed our new apartment. I went to school and worked a part-time job. I was bright, independent, and respectful to all. Shing also went to a Catholic boys school, and I met his extended family and his friends. When he was old enough to work, I hooked him up at the store where he began just as I did, making deliveries on the weekends and then working inside the store. We had a great experience working together.

Shing's mother would lend us her car because my stepbrother was a good driver and had been driving for a while without incident. We went to parties with our own transportation rather than using the subway or spending money on taxis. This was more convenient than trying to catch a taxi or a ride from a friend when the party was over. All we had to do was to be careful and to make sure the gas tank was full after we used the car. That was easy for us because we pooled our money. My stepbrother could drive all day if necessary. He seemed born to drive, and he loved doing it.

It turned out that a person living on our street was working for that television conglomerate. Mr. B, a Jamaican expatriate, introduced me to his coworkers and was instrumental in getting me a summer job at the station. My stepbrother was the first to get a job there because he was the oldest and was followed in succession by me and Shing. We were always looking out for each other. Some jokingly called us the three musketeers, but that is how it should be for people growing up together. We didn't have to be blood brothers, but we were brothers in Christ Jesus. We all went to Catholic school, but we weren't thinking about our friendship in Christ at the time. We just considered ourselves boys who lived and hung out together.

I graduated from high school with second honors but not without controversy amid the euphoria. After my graduation Mr. B got me the summer job in an entry-level department. I had mobility because that position took me to many offices. This afforded me the opportunity to see and interface with others. Although the contact was minimal at times, it allowed me to plant seeds for the future.

In the eighteen months or so before graduation, my friendship with one of the girls I met in that group of teenagers grew. She was beautiful and we were friends while she dated other guys. We would make fun of her over her first boyfriend. He lived in another state and would drive down with a carload of friends, country boys caught in a fashion time warp. They had processed hair, do rags on their heads, high-water pants pulled up to the mid-stomach, and pointed shoes. They were supposed to be a singing group but appeared to be a bunch of Little Richards with a 1950s look in 1968. They shunned the Afros and the dashikis that spoke of pride in blackness and the struggle for recognition. In their ignorance or defiance of style, they unwittingly screamed, "Oh no, we won't join," and so they stood out like sore thumbs.

My girlfriend and I began our relationship in close proximity to each other, but she could not visit me when no adults were home. I followed the rules. I was mostly down the street whenever I was not in my house. We hung out in Wally's garage, harmonizing as a singing group, and in De De's walk-in basement, playing records, practicing dance steps, watching television, or catching up on some kissing. When we were not in the basement or the garage we hung out by the gates of someone's house. Wally lived next door to Mr. Been, and Mr. Been lived next door to De De. On the other side of Wally was Mr. Tors and then Mr. B's house. There were a few other houses in the middle, and then there was Shing's house where my family lived on the top floor. Shing's mom was a cool lady, so we got along well and there were no restrictions on my friends and me going up or down the stairs to hang out with each other.

When we hung out in front we were in clear view, so our parents could look up or down the street and shout for us to come home. Wally was a junior because his father's name was Wally as well. It was Wally who had the dog being walked around the block when I first saw this group of people. Much later on De De's mom got a poodle that had to be walked. Wally would walk his dog at night, and if we were outside, he would put the dog inside and hang out for a while. Whenever we were at Wally's house at night his mom would stick her head out of the second-floor window and call him in. Wally's parents were older than my parents. Wally was a late arrival, so his mother's voice sounded a bit shriller than the others. So picture this row of two-story brick houses. You are a teenager trying to be cool with the girls and the dudes, and your mother opens the window, sticks her head out, and yells, "Wally Jr., it's ten o'clock. Come inside!" She would do that to him continually, and we would crack up. Sometimes when it was getting close to nine we would make jokes regarding Wally's impending ten o'clock call to bed. We would tell him he'd better get inside by nine before he got a whipping. He was a good sport, though.

We did not go out on school nights but only on weekend nights and during the summer. We were good kids and none of us got into major trouble, but back at my house life was becoming quite sticky. My stepbrother was about to move away because he and his girlfriend were expecting and they were getting married. He gave up school. His mother was greatly disappointed because he was her only son, and she hoped he would finish school and move on to greater things. My father was disappointed as well, and now the plot thickened.

I began to hear criticism for having a girlfriend. I was told this would affect my school performance, my ability to graduate, and my future in general. My stepmother said she was tired of trying to keep food warmed for me in the evenings and so she wasn't going to do that anymore. My personal things began to disappear, and when I asked if anyone had removed an item, I was told, "No. Maybe you misplaced it, so look again where you left it."

I had been working the full twenty hours allowed each week and got a split-week schedule so I would be off two days during the week and would always work on the most important days, Friday and Saturday. I had been working for years, and all my stepmom had to do was leave dinner in the refrigerator, the oven, or on top of the stove as she always had. I had not asked her to do anything else, because I worked till nine o'clock and I was home by ten unless there was a subway delay. If I was not hungry, I placed the dinner in the refrigerator. She was not up keeping food warm as she claimed, but after a while she stopped leaving dinner when I worked during the week. I didn't care. I made sure I ate while I was at work.

I was working for many reasons, and the first was that I wanted to maintain a certain independence. I lived in the home that my parents provided, but I helped with a contribution they asked me to make each time I got paid. I paid for my tuition after my first two freshman semesters all the way to graduation. I bought my own clothes and shoes and whatever else I needed. And finally, I sent money to Jamaica to my biological mother to help her care for herself and for my brothers and my sister. My oldest brother was working in Jamaica and later became a mechanic at the US navy base in Guantanamo Bay, Cuba, so between us we provided the help she needed.

My biological mother and I corresponded often enough for me to know what was transpiring in my family, and I remember at sixteen telling her I would help take care of her. "Don't worry about not having a husband," I said. She had not been successful in relationships, and since her stepfather had died, it seemed as though the little she had was up for grabs. Her parents had died without a will, and since her stepfather was not her biological father, the property had to be probated and left open to all challenges. There were seven. She had to refute all seven before she could be awarded the property as the rightful heir. My mother needed money to cover filing and processing fees, and the situation was not resolved for many years. Jamaican law was derived from the British legal system.

When I began to notice that my personal things were disappearing, my stepmother was becoming close to the wife of a friend of my parents. They became so close that they took a trip to Jamaica by themselves. The friend was Jamaican, and although the trip seemed innocent, it had a sinister purpose. A secret cargo represented an attack on my well-being and a violation of God's moral code. I had lost a comb, a toothbrush, a hairbrush, a belt, underwear, a special shirt given to me by my girlfriend, samples of my writing, and schoolwork.

Although my stepbrother was now living in another city we kept in touch. His wife was beautiful and a cool person, so we got along well. I had been discussing the changes in our parents and how the two of them were pressuring me, and my stepbrother and his wife were there for me when I needed them. In the summer I could work many hours beyond twenty whenever I was needed at the store, and I did this because I was saving to buy an engagement ring for my girlfriend. We went ring shopping at jewelry stores, selected a ring, and had it sized. I put a down payment on it and was having it engraved. I told my parents the news, and they were not happy at all. My girlfriend's mom and stepfather had no objections. They were happy that I was making a commitment to her, but my father told me that I had to get out of his house by the end of the month.

He said that two bulls could not reign in one pen. I thought he was behaving irrationally. He could have said, "Son, I understand you love her, but make this a long engagement and take time to see where this is eventually going. You are both young, and you need time to make the right decisions." Instead, he took the low road.

My stepmother did not like my girlfriend but pretended she did. My girlfriend was beautiful, her mother was beautiful, and to make things worse her mother did not socialize with the other adults on the block. She would say hello, but she would go upstairs to her apartment, spend time with her husband and her children, get into her car and go to work or to shop, and that was it. My stepmother always claimed that my girlfriend's mom thought she was better than everybody else. My stepmother was loud and liked to party, quite the opposite from my girlfriend's mom. She was a churchgoer, and after going out with my girlfriend for a while I began to attend church with her on Sundays. Nobody went to church in my house, so I guess this was an added slap in the face as far as my parents were concerned. I would be gone all day Sunday with my girlfriend and her mother. I would sometimes have Sunday dinner at her grandma's house with most of her family after church.

The end of the month arrived, and on a Sunday evening around five o'clock I was lying on my bed while my parents were in their room. My father left his room, got his tools, and entered my room. He took apart my brother's old bed and leaned it up against the wall and then came over to my bed, grabbed the mattress, and heaved me onto the floor. He stood over me and began disassembling the bed. The remainder of the evening's events were ugly and shameful. My stepmom was screaming her head off and calling for Shing and his mother to come upstairs. Shing arrived first and tried to stop us from battling by calling out to my father. But what got my attention was his mother calling out, "Nathan, don't fight your father." I froze.

My landlady asked me to go downstairs to cool off and I did. I called my stepbrother and told him and his wife what had happened, and he said, "Just get out of there, and I'll pick you up from downstairs. You can stay with us." That's what I did. Several days passed, and I continued going to school and to work. My stepmom kept calling, but I did not take the calls to speak to either of them. Around the end of the week my parents called and spoke to my stepbrother, and he told me, "Just take the call and see what they have to say." They were sorry and wanted me to come home, so after a few more days I decided to try again. My stepbrother drove me back to the house.

I would not give my father the satisfaction of knowing that he had hurt me. I was determined to succeed despite the odds I was facing, and I would not be a failure as my parents were predicting. I heard that I would not graduate from high school, that I had become worthless, and that they were sorry they had brought me up from Jamaica. These were things I was told before our dust-up that evening. The pot had been percolating and the Devil had turned up the heat.

I graduated from high school with second honors. The graduation exercises were held in a college auditorium, and my stepmom told me that when I walked across the stage and received my diploma, my father sat with his chest out and said, "My son. That's my son." She mocked him. They threw me a graduation party on the weekend, and it sure was a great celebration! But why would a father be so misled about his one and only biological son? Looking back, I see that he had allowed himself to discard God's protective covering. There was no worship in the house, and no one went to church. I don't know whether my farther even remembered individual prayer as a way to have a relationship with God. During that period, I never saw him bowed down and praying. The Devil is cunning. Be ever vigilant!

Graduating into Adulthood

Our neighbor Mr. B arranged for me to speak to his boss about a summer job, and I took him up on the opportunity after graduation. I began working at this communications company and got to see the television production areas including newsrooms, control rooms, studios, film and videotape facilities, and editing suites. I was amazed that I had been sitting at home watching television when God directed me to this career path and that I was now at a television station, being introduced to these facilities. God is a miracle worker.

My job allowed me to enter newsrooms where I saw reporters, writers, and anchors. I got to meet people all over the broadcast complex as I took films to viewing rooms, retrieved them for return shipment, supplied empty film canisters to the newsroom, and picked up film canisters for the archives. I also visited offices big and small to carry out minor tasks. Such operations have departments with specific jobs, and to move beyond the set boundaries is an encroachment. The building, however, had to be kept free of spills and overflowing trash on days when the contracted cleaning staff was not on duty. We also made sure the rest rooms were supplied and cleaned. The regular cleaning staff did the full cleaning during the night hours. I secured friendships with film and tape editors, producers, writers, and other general office workers.

When summer ended, my boss looked for a way to keep me on as a full-time employee, so he assigned me to the four-p.m.-to-midnight shift, allowing me to take classes during the days. The country was in a recession and my company was cutting back. The people I worked with knew I was heading to college and tried to help in any way they could. They were able to keep me working until October of 1970, and then I was laid off. My boss promised that when the opportunity arose, he would take me back if I chose to return. I remembered that promise when it was time to reapply.

I enrolled at a college with a four-year liberal arts program that I could leave after my junior year for a degree program in broadcast communications. I did not like the set-up because I would get to do what I wanted only in the last year. I had been considering a school of television production and directing but followed my parents' advice and chose a four-year college. My father hoped to live vicariously through me, telling me he wanted me to be an engineer. I did not have that desire. My focus was on television, and so I dropped out of college after the Thanksgiving break in November.

My girlfriend and I had gone through with the engagement and were inseparable. In October we found out that we were expecting. We went to her parents and told them the news, and I assured them that we were not considering an abortion. That was out of the question, I said. I would take care of her, and we wanted to get married. They told me they weren't expecting news of the pregnancy, but they knew that I was a stable young man who desired to do the best for their daughter, so they agreed to the marriage. Next, I went to my parents alone and explained the situation. They wouldn't agree to a marriage, so my fiancée and I planned to go to a state where we could get married without permission from my parents.

Soon after, we moved to an apartment on the fourth floor of a four-story walk-up. We had a sublet agreement and shared with another couple. We chose Delaware to get married since it was the closest and the most affordable state for travel, hotel, food, and fees. We made the arrangements and spent a romantic weekend in Delaware where we got married and then returned home to our state. Since I had lost the summer job at the communications company I had been interviewing and sending résumes but had found nothing acceptable, so I returned to work at a place where I had a track record. I had worked in a supermarket since my sixteenth birthday, and the job was not beneath me now that I was a high school graduate. I needed a job and had no time to fool around; I was a young man with a wife and a child on the way.

While working in the supermarket during high school, I was fortunate to have gotten a higher pay rate per hour than many coworkers. I had mastered the art of creating and building fancy displays and could arrange and stock shelf space with speed, spotlighting products. I remained in that job for a year, and then I got an opportunity to work as a statistical clerk under a federal program in the Department of Health. Before accepting this job, I had to face a few issues that God worked out in my favor. The military draft instituted because of the Vietnam War was still in place, and I was called to report for active duty. Before being called up, I had visited the doctor for diagnosis and treatment. Stress had caused me to develop a stomach ulcer. I was put on limited medication, but most of all I had to watch what I ate and drank. Due to this stomach ulcer and a mild nervous condition, I escaped induction into the armed forces and was reclassified as medically unfit.

We became proud parents of a little girl who did not like to sleep at night. She would sleep for short periods, wake up, and then try to stay up for what seemed like forever. I shared the care of our child in the evenings after work, and this was taxing because I did manual labor during the day. We were young, and my wife wanted me to stay up late at night to keep her company since I was gone all day. One salary had to cover everything for a while. I got a part-time job in the evenings that added a little more money.

For the first time in many years, my wife had no separate spring clothing collection that was distinguishable from her summer collection. She had been used to having her seasons separated by clothing lines, so that did not sit well with her. Picture an audience seated in a big tent at New York's Fashion Week extravaganza or maybe in Paris or Milan, waiting for all of the new and exciting designs, only to have the emcee announce that no new designs will be unveiled this season. After a loud gasp, people say, "You are kidding? Tell me that's a joke!" That was the reaction in our household when I made the same announcement. A woman's figure changes after she gives birth, but we also had to rule out other things as being unaffordable.

It seemed as soon as we had a small stretch of peace, we had to have some disruption. About six months after our daughter was born a pipe began leaking in the kitchen wall. The plumbing was such that repair workers had to rip out part of the kitchen wall by the sink and continue into the bathroom just above the bathtub. They fixed the leak because water was seeping into the ceiling of the apartment below us and had caused a partial cave-in, but they never came back to repair our walls. We kept after them until we decided to move. We were afraid that a mouse might come out of the broken wall and bite our beloved daughter in her crib.

These things seemed to happen one after the other, and when my stepmother heard about our dilemma, she told me to come back home to live. There were two empty bedrooms since my brother and I had moved out. I had to consider this offer before I accepted it. When I moved out to marry my girlfriend, my dad told me never to return to his house. After several months had passed, my stepmother sent a message to my stepbrother telling me I had important mail at her house. When I went to pick up the mail, my dad came home and asked me bluntly, "Didn't I tell you not to come back here?" I quickly answered, "I came to get my mail." He replied, "Okay, take your mail and go."

I had not intended to linger when I got there, but my stepmom asked me to sit down to talk. "How is everything?" she wanted to know. "How is your wife? Do you want something to eat? You look thin." After this encounter with my dad I stayed away until after our daughter was born. I called and spoke to my stepmom to give her news of the birth. Then I went to the house to give my parents a picture of the baby that was taken in the hospital. I also handed out cigars to the people I knew on the block.

My wife did not want to stay with my parents, so she went to live with her biological father for a few months. He had a large house occupied just by him and his brother. I would stay there over the weekend after spending weekdays with my parents, but I did not like the atmosphere. Getting to work from there in the mornings also involved too much travel because there were no direct routes.

Looking back on how and why I returned to my father's house, I see two explanations. First, some people want to see proof that their misdeeds have affected lives, and others want to play the rescuer in the situations they created. Second, God is present in every situation. He the God of Abraham, Isaac, and Jacob, the God for all who accept Jesus Christ as their Lord and Savior. He is always ready to offer His blessings and to change all things for the good of those who love Him (Romans 8:28).

After a few months without me during the week, my wife decided she would come to my parents' house so we could be together. We stayed there for a short while and then rented a place month to month in an adjoining county. We lived on the ground floor with a single young lady who worked in finance and with another young couple. The owner and his sons lived on the top floor. Soon after, we got a large apartment in a two-family house, and I returned to school to pursue my instruction in television production and directing. My wife started secretarial classes and got a job, but within months, things began to unravel.

I was attending classes four days a week in the evenings after working full days, so I usually did not get home until at least ten o'clock. I left for work at six-thirty in the morning. I did this for eleven months to graduate from the program on the fast track. About midway into my school program, my wife signed up for modeling classes with a group promising to make professional models out of young ladies. She attended the classes in the evenings and was soon going to shows on the weekends. Our daughter was my priority, and I made sure I spent all my free time with her. As for my wife and me, our priorities had changed and we grew apart. We couldn't agree on the best way to guarantee success for both of us and to maintain a relationship, so we separated, agreeing that I would not be limited in spending time with our daughter.

My success was paramount, and even before my marriage crumbled, I was nearing a return to the communications profession. A position had opened up at my old company, and I could work in the same department, though at a different location. I resigned from my job as a statistical clerk and returned to the communications company. I forged a relationship with a brother who served as a mentor and helped me navigate the corporate structure. He was in middle management, and even though my aim was to be in production, his insight and advice were invaluable.

About three months later I was able to return to the main production facilities where my destiny awaited. My boss soon outfitted me with a beeper so I could check for job assignments rather than trek down to the office each time I was needed. This main facility was a vast structure with ample production and office space. I became familiar with every inch of that place while working there. In between making my rounds and answering assignment calls, I found quiet spaces to read and to study. As an employee, I also had access to the research library and read everything I could concerning television production.

When the soaps were being produced, I would go above the studio floor and observe from the catwalks. I watched the rehearsals, the floor blocking, and sometimes the live tapings. The lighting techs were familiar with me, and I was always quiet so no one else knew I was there. I knew people in wardrobe, props, and set decorations, so I was also in those departments observing and comparing what

I was taught and what I read against what I saw. Soon I was in film editing rooms and videotape bays observing recordings, editing, and playbacks. Early in this process I met the film editor and assistant to a respected and popular personality, and he introduced me to his boss. I told the editor that I was attending classes and wanted to be in production, and his boss said I could hang around anytime except when they were on deadline. I made full use of that offer because most of my questions pertained to film editing.

As soon as I graduated from school, I began visiting the personnel office to make my intentions known. I had been keeping an eye on the jobs board outside the office. I knew that I could type only twenty words a minute on a manual typewriter. The requirements for most internal entry-level hires were completion of at least six months in one's present position and the ability to type thirty-five words a minute on the IBM electric typewriter. I had the six months, but I had to learn how to use the IBM typewriter and to increase my speed to thirty-five words a minute. I did not have an IBM electric typewriter at home. They were expensive. So I gave up half of my lunch hour each day and practiced on the typewriter in the personnel office, the one used to give speed tests.

After being at the company for about a year and a half, I got my break. I was hired as a news clerk in a department connected to news production. The department functioned as a production library for the news division, handling the supply and housing of all news videotape stocks, pre-production videotape materials, and all news broadcast program tapes in various stages. We also handled edited masters and post-production materials.

As my marriage was failing, another aspect of God's promise was coming into bloom. Perhaps as you are beginning to make progress toward a cherished goal, other facets of your life are falling apart. There are some things we can't control despite our best efforts, but the God who made us will work them out for the best. When my wife and I had come to an end, I felt great pain and disappointment. Without the strength and the promise of God, I could have been driven to actions that were against His will. Recall that when I was a boy of five or six, my grandfather's friend had prophesied that I would travel to America, have a hard life, and be married four times but would be successful and be a ruler.

Being a ruler does not necessarily mean to rule as a king or a president but to have charge over others, perhaps as a manager or a supervisor. Most of all it means to rule under God's grace over the onslaught of Satan.

My first wife and I were married in the fall of 1970 and by late spring of 1973 had stopped living as man and wife. She moved to another county, and I tried to put some distance between myself and the hurt I was feeling. I moved in with my stepbrother, his wife, and their daughter and lived with them while I rebuilt my life. I always kept in contact with my former wife because of our daughter and was in good standing with her mom and her stepfather. I fulfilled all of my responsibilities to our daughter because I loved her and loved being with her.

God has acted through several of these people to meet pressing needs I was facing. I don't think they recognized that it was God who caused them to reach out, but I know. As for my first wife, God moved in my life as well as her family's life. Some forty-two years after our breakup, God nudged me to let her know that when we began our relationship, He was there. No one in my house was going to church, but God caused this woman and her family to allow me to accompany them to church on Sundays. Through them I was able to gain God's favor with worship and praise.

My friend Shing and I lost contact around 1983 and did not speak to or see each other until 2014. But God had a plan for us just as He has a plan for each person He has created. All we have to do is stay with Him and do His will so He can use us to fulfill His plan. My stepbrother and I had also lost contact after 1995, but through the urging of the Spirit of God I looked him up and reached out to him. I will connect all of these stories later.

Moving Forward in My Career and in Love

I moved from my stepbrother's home in 1975, renting a first-floor apartment in a building close to a subway line and a shopping area. I did a lot of work in that apartment, painting it, scraping the wooden parquet floors, staining them with a beautiful clear gloss, and fumigating the place. Before completing all of the decorations, I met a beautiful and charming young lady who was visiting from Great Britain. She was ending a summer visit with her parents and her family and was about to return home. We had a great time talking and spending time with her family in the few days before she flew back to England. She told me and others that when she returned to England she and her boyfriend planned to get engaged, but things did not turn out that way. He was not ready to commit to her, though she had given an ultimatum since they had been together for a long time. He wanted to go to the Middle East to work in the oil fields and was hoping to receive a contract at any moment.

We met in July, and at the end of August she called to tell me that things did not turn out as she had hoped but that she had been unable to get me out of her mind. Her parents, who had relocated from England to America, had been trying to convince her to return, but they were unsuccessful. After exchanging a few telephone calls, she told me she now wanted to leave England and come to America permanently but not to live with her parents. She wanted to be with me, and if I would agree to this arrangement, she would wrap up her business there, get some stuff shipped, and fly back since a visa had been granted before all of this took place. I said that this would be okay and that I looked forward to having her with me. And that is how we began, each person wanting to forget the past and to forge ahead with a new and exciting union.

She was very creative, designing and sewing her own clothes, and was also a trained chef. She began immediately to make curtains and pillows, decorating the apartment with eclectic pieces that were just right. We had gourmet meals and fine wine, lit candles, and multiple courses. We were young and searching for love, climbing ladders to success, socializing, and exploring the city's culture and history, but soon there would be a bump in the road. She was used to being a big fish in a small pond, and being in a mega city changed that. In England she won many cooking and sewing competitions, was featured in the local newspaper, and did radio interviews. She was also an aspiring Afro contemporary dancer who had made several appearances with her dance troupe. In America she was just a talented and beautiful young lady who had not yet gotten much recognition beyond that of family and friends. She did not know how to handle that situation gracefully and with patience.

She had some successes, but they were not the individual successes she had imagined with the same hoopla as before, and to complicate things I had a more prestigious job. She loved attention and tried to gain the spotlight at all times. If she was introducing herself or was asked her name, she would proudly state her first and her middle names. That was how she wanted to be known. She wanted everyone to acknowledge the uncommonness of her first name and the beauty of the flower associated with her middle name. She was my beautiful dark chocolate flower and was very strong and determined but was also delicate and brittle.

We traded up from that first apartment into a larger and more comfortable one, and she was delighted to decorate it. I had received two promotions for my hard work since she had returned from England, the first to supervising news clerk and the second to production assistant. My chocolate rose was working as a receptionist/intake clerk in a family clinic, not in her field as a chef, and was thoroughly bored with the job within a short while and wanted out. We had been looking for an opportunity in her field but found nothing appealing until we saw an ad for a head chef for a new restaurant in a trendy part of the city.

My flower interviewed and was hired on the spot as the restaurant's first employee, but she was soon disappointed. The managers had picked her brain to help them to set up and get ready for inspection and the grand opening, but they had given the head chef position to someone else. They kept her on as their utility chef. They used her to do everything since she was trained and experienced in preparing French cuisine. Though she was now working in her field, she was often aggravated because she felt used and lied to by people she still had to deal with and further insulted because the others had much less talent and knowledge than she possessed. We agreed that she would remain just to build a résumé of American experience and move on at the first opportunity.

Later she wanted to enroll in school for a degree in fashion design, and I agreed since she had been so disillusioned with the food industry and wanted to exploit her other talent. I agreed, realizing she needed an outlet to explore her abilities since she became depressed at times and cried over things present and past. I began to see a pattern of behavior that was affecting me in many ways. She blamed me for her issues and began to second-guess her decision to come to America. She cried about events from her childhood, her teenage years, and her adult years, and she cried because I failed to marry her. She cried about the appearance of my first wife because when my flower was a child, such girls were considered pretty, and when she was a teenager boys went out with such girls while they overlooked her.

She cried that kids teased her when she was young and had a blood condition that caused her to bruise easily and to form scabs. She cried that my daughter looked so much like her mother, light-skinned, pretty, and with long hair. She cried because she thought that maybe I loved my first wife more than I loved her. She cried because she said all I cared about was my career, because she said I was a bore, and because she thought I was having affairs at work since she found telephone numbers in my pocket. I had telephone numbers in my pockets because I called many people, usually to get my job done. Normally I kept their numbers on a clipboard, but sometimes in my haste I put the numbers on slips of paper that I shoved into my pockets.

I had a female contact in Washington, D.C., with whom I would exchange information to facilitate our broadcasts. My flower got a hold of her telephone number, called her, and pretended to be a police detective, saying that I was in an accident, that I was unresponsive, and that the only contact number I had on me was hers. The obvious question followed: "What is your relationship with him?" So you can see what was happening. She was building up to a breakdown but was refusing to acknowledge the real problem. She kept telling me that I was to blame because I had not gotten a divorce and asked her to marry me. She said I was taking the easy way out and using her.

At the time, I did not know her complete medical status, so I could not say for sure that she was having a breakdown or that one was imminent. I took to heart her complaint that I was still married and had not married her, so I obtained a divorce, and we got engaged and set a wedding date. I do not want to paint an unfair picture. My flower was not simply a chronic complainer. She challenged me in every way to be better and more adventurous. We were once part of a four-person group that managed a huge ballroom. The owner was looking for someone to take it over and bring new life and profitability to the operation, and my flower challenged me to do this in addition to my regular job in production.

We did this successfully for about a year but got fed up with the other two people, who did not want to do any of the physical work it took to run the place. They just wanted to have meetings, get dressed up, and introduce themselves as the management group while we did all of the grunt work. My flower and I withdrew from the group. The other two tried to carry on but failed. My flower had the hospitality expertise while I had the production knowledge and business acumen.

As a production assistant, I had a more demanding schedule than before. I was promoted in 1976, a presidential election year, and many other major events took place over the next few years, so I spent an enormous amount of time at work. To be engaged in other ventures was quite taxing for me and for my flower. She was working as a chef during the day and managing the ballroom on the weekends. She also started a little catering business in our apartment, making cakes for weddings and other occasions. Whenever I was home I pitched in to help her get things done.

During that time, I worked primarily on the morning show, so I was at work at four a.m. and back home by 11 a.m. if it was a normal morning without major events. Otherwise I might return at 2 or 4 p.m. Sometimes I would not come home but would stay in a hotel until the following day because of breaking news. There were times when I would have to stay to help staff other taped or live news productions. I sometimes covered the Saturday, Sunday evening, and Sunday night editions, but I still had not reached my goal: to be assigned to the show I was watching when the Spirit of the Lord came upon me. I eventually succeeded, but I had to fight because some were intent on stopping me. Satan was working through them, but I continued to work toward my goal and tried to bring more harmony at home.

In 1978 my flower and I got married. Expressive and competitive person that she was, she designed and made her own wedding dress, the bridesmaids' and the flower girls' dresses, and our wedding cake and did all of the wedding planning. She handed over the catering to a trusted friend who was also a chef. Attendees came from England, Canada, Jamaica, and several US states. We honeymooned in Montego Bay, Jamaica, and traveled around the island to meet each other's extended families. Returning home, we again pursued our professional goals. A new position became available at a five-star French restaurant in midtown, and she made her exit from the other establishment. She felt she was moving closer to her career goals, but school was becoming more taxing on her. She had to produce an increasing number of designs but was frustrated with her sketching abilities and got little sleep most days because of schoolwork.

We decided to take a vacation during her spring semester in 1979, and we took a trip to England with the possibility of visiting France as well. We stayed in London for a week and then traveled around the Midlands, and the area where my flower had grown up, for two weeks. During our week in London, we decided to forget about France and do some shopping in London and elsewhere. In addition, I got some dental work done. There was a nice Indian family whose son had a dental practice and was highly recommended. I agreed to pay him a small upfront fee and to forward the remaining payment in American dollars to his family in India. He did great work that lasted for many years, and I sent his family the agreed-upon amount with a little extra. Dental work was far less expensive in England than in America, at least at the time.

While in the Midlands, we discovered that a beauty pageant was about to take place and that there was still time for contestants to register. My wife, who was of West Indian heritage and still a British subject, decided to enter. She told me she was certain to win the crown, and she did. On the night of the contest she was interviewed for radio and sat for pictures for a local newspaper. She was stylish, personable, and stunning, but she sometimes behaved very badly.

A few of her relatives in England said she appeared to be out of control. I began to see the possibility of a breakdown when one of her older sisters, who had to seek treatment, advised her to do the same. However, my flower was in total denial that anything remotely like that could happen to her. She told me that her sister's condition was due to mental and physical abuse by her former husband, who was jailed for mistreating her. My wife insisted she did not have a similar problem. I pondered this development but decided not to pursue it and to see where events would lead.

We returned home and resumed our routines, but things were changing. I had sought changes in my work assignments and I got them. Since my promotion to program production assistant in 1976, I had been assigned primarily to the morning show but had the opportunity to work on other shows when the need arose or I campaigned for an assignment. I had observed all of the politics and the assignments of a certain class of people and had decided that I needed to be more visible so that more producers and directors would appreciate my abilities and my dedication. I felt this would catapult me to the spot I wanted. My goal was still very much alive, and I was determined to achieve it.

I had earlier met with someone of note in news operations and had told this person I had paid my dues on the morning show and wanted to be assigned elsewhere. I had gotten the usual runaround. My services to the show were invaluable, this person said, and I was needed there. Everyone was aware of the work I was doing, and I didn't need to go anywhere else. I needed to be more patient. After all, I had gotten several promotions over the last few years.

In effect, I was being told, "We hired you and since then we have promoted you several times. You are going too far in requesting meetings and trying to throw your weight around. You can't tell us what to do, so just be grateful and shut up. We will do things the way we want to do them."

At the time most of those hired in the entry-level department I began, were black men who usually stayed with the department throughout their work tenures. I knew of only a few who were elevated, and this probably happened because of passage and enforcement of equal employment legislation in the 1960s. Although company executives could not say plainly what they meant, a young white man told me how he felt about my promotions. He said, "Nathan, you ought to write a book titled *Porter to Production and Program Production Assistant.*"

A porter in the minds of many people is a black man with no brains who is unfit to do anything but mop floors and clean up after whites. He is supposed to remain subservient and be grateful that they have allowed him to have this menial job to feed his family. This fellow who addressed me was ticked off because he had been promoted to program production assistant, had made a complete fool of himself, and had been demoted. He'd gotten the assignment I aspired to have. He had to return to a department where I was his supervisor, and he hated that. Several months later, I got promoted to program production assistant, a highly sought and highly competitive position. This man gave me his unwanted advice after I had survived a six-month probationary period and was excelling, contrary to his expectation.

In many large corporations, people have started in the mailroom and have worked their way to the top, but some saw my company's entry-level department as inferior since it was staffed mainly by black men. But I pray in all situations, and I encourage you to do the same. I used to have several New Testament pocket Bibles, and I carried one at all times in my jacket, my pants, or in a leather shoulder bag. Since I spent so many hours at work and sometimes had to stay overnight, I had one stashed in a toiletries case in my locker. I did not care if anybody knew, because I prayed continually silently or reading Scripture. I had my weapon of choice with me, for I believed that the God who kept Israel would neither leave me nor forsake me.

The fact that I was still assigned to the morning show and wasn't getting a fair shake remained paramount on my mind, so after returning from England I scheduled a meeting with a senior person in operations. I respectfully told that person what was on my mind and asked to be reassigned. Later I was reassigned but way out in left field where management thought I would not be used much. This would be punishment for my audacity. I was assigned to the cultural affairs unit, but that assignment worked wonderfully to advance my plans despite management's expectations. When God is with you and has ordained your steps, who can defeat you? (Romans 8:31).

While I was winning this victory in the workplace, my home life was disintegrating. My flower had grown distant with her focus on work and school, but there were added factors. She had cut and twisted her hair, vowing not to perm it again. She was smoking marijuana more frequently, had become a vegetarian, and was espousing the Rastafarian creed. I was not upset that she wanted to wear her hair in a dreadlock style, but she had gone overboard in idolizing Bob Marley and in smoking weed. She wanted us to give up our apartment for a more central place in the city, but I told her that I liked our refuge and that we needed to save money rather than to pay exorbitant amounts for rent. She strongly disagreed. Our trip to England had cost almost four thousand dollars, not including my dental expenses, and we needed to replenish that sum before we considered more debt. But that was not a factor for her. She wanted to move. She was not happy.

I said that a move to the middle of the city would not solve our issues because we had grown miles apart and because she wouldn't admit that she needed medical help. About a month later we had an argument, and I left the apartment for several hours. When I came home, she had taken a whole bottle of aspirin. I tried to induce vomiting and called emergency services to take her to the hospital. I remained with her as she spent the night under observation. She was given follow-up information and instructions that she ignored. She continued in denial until that was impossible.

Soon after, she and a friend agreed to share an apartment, and they found one overlooking a trendy avenue on the Upper East Side. I told her she could take anything for her apartment except my personal stuff. She took whatever she wanted and left only a few pieces of furniture. I was hurt but decided I would survive. She continued to insist that she was rational, and some of her words rang in my ears long after she was gone. I knew they were not true. She told me that I was at fault for our failed relationship, just as I had been responsible when my first marriage did not work, and that I was the one who needed professional help. If you are not a strong and secure person, such accusations can change you for the worse, but for me, the wisdom of God was greater than the wisdom of man.

My wife settled into her apartment but at times had to seek help to pay the rent and the utilities. Her friend was a waitress and depended largely on tips. Sometimes the money was not there, so my wife asked for cash and for food. About ten months after moving, she had a blowup with her boyfriend at her apartment and lost it completely. She stabbed him and then smashed a few windows facing the street. Emergency services came and promptly took her to a psychiatric facility for observation and treatment.

The young man did not press charges, and her roommate cleaned up the apartment. I got someone to fix the damaged windows and visited my wife in the psychiatric facility. It was heart-rending to see her drugged up and lethargic. My beautiful, talented, and vibrant flower had drowned in the tidal waves of life and self. Lord Jesus, help us to surmount our unbelief and to grab hold of Your nail-scarred hand, for there is no other way to the Father than through You. Bob Marley was not God!

My wife was released from the hospital after about a week. We stayed married but did not get back together. This arrangement helped her and her family, but a few years later I found another woman and needed to free myself to move on. She continued in and out of institutions for the rest of her life, having been diagnosed as manic depressive, bipolar, and schizophrenic. She has left us. A flower exhibits its beauty today and tomorrow is no more, withered away. We can thank God, though, for the knowledge and experience He shared with us.

My career had to compete with my personal and marital issues, but when Christ is in the vessel you smile at the storm and keep moving. You might have to shift the sails or take them down and paddle, but you can survive and reach the shore, so I made all of the necessary adjustments, finding ways to deal with my pain and my disappointment. Besides praying, I began spending time in deep meditation and cleansing when I was home. I did not run out to buy new furniture or appliances to replace what was taken. I became a minimalist. I had to maintain my core values to handle events that could easily have overcome me if I had no faith or works.

I became a program production assistant in 1976, the bicentennial anniversary of the United States. Large celebrations were planned all over the nation for July Fourth, and I had much work to do that day. Our station went on to win an Emmy Award for coverage of the bicentennial. Since I worked on the show, I shared the Emmy credit.

After my assignment to the cultural affairs department, I was blessed to share in another Emmy Award. The winning series was complex, and my ability to handle this production opened many eyes. When one man is playing many characters, many rehearsals and costume and script changes are required to keep track of countless scenes, takes, and retakes. Someone must record time measurements, know where everything is located, and spend long hours in the editing room until the product is completed. I was grateful to be there while all of this was happening, because there had been times when the department had gone on hiatus and didn't need a long-term program production assistant.

God had laid the groundwork when I had that epiphany while watching the evening news in the summer of 1969. Under the influence of demonic forces, men are always attempting to derail God's plan for us. Sometimes they are fully aware of what drives them to do the things they do, and at other times they have no clue, but God is always able to do what He says He will do.

After a whirlwind of production in the cultural affairs department, there was a lull and I had much time on my hands with no show assigned. I was on call for any assignment that became available, but waiting was time lost as far as I was concerned. I devised a plan to get myself assigned to the most coveted news program and began by approaching the show's director and program production assistant. I told the director that I wanted to observe the program production assistant during the daily pre-production and broadcast and then on slow news days gradually relieve that person of duties until I could relieve him completely. That person would then be able to observe associate directors for additional training.

My proposal went over well because our bargaining unit had a contract provision that allowed the opportunity to prepare for advancement to associate director. The first step was usually observation and the next was performance. Under this arrangement, I could help out the news program when I had no show assignments. I knew that when the director asked the schedule manager for me, the request would be approved. The broadcast was prestigious, and God always makes a way! I did not need the observation time and training on the news program, because I was familiar with every aspect of the job and the show, but I had to demonstrate to the director that I could handle the responsibilities without incident. The executive producer and producers had to be confident in me as well. This was the desired opportunity initiated on that day in 1969.

I was filling in regularly on the program and showcasing my talents for my next move, applying for a promotion to associate director. I had done the morning show for years along with the weekend edition of the evening news, news specials, and the cultural programs. On many occasions I was used as a stage manager, filling in until a staff stage manager could take over. I had also had bit assignments classified under our contract as associate director's duties. Each time I worked at a higher level of responsibility, I got higher pay and more credits toward my goal of becoming an associate director.

A new show was planned, and I knew that it would need staffing, including associate directors. I applied for an associate director's position but was passed over. Since this remained an opportunity, I decided that I would seek an assignment on the show as a production assistant. The show's premiere was a success, and the program is still on the air today. I wound up working as a program production assistant and as an associate director on upgrade most of the time.

Those successes enhanced my résumé as I moved toward my goal, but my path forward remained blocked. My schedule was such that I was no longer able to volunteer for the evening news or be scheduled for the show. The powers that be were trying to shut the door on me. I could never get away from the morning show since I was always being scheduled to take over someone's assignment. Those working other daytime shows or the evening news viewed this program as the graveyard shift. As I kept being assigned to the morning show revamp after revamp, I saw it the same way.

I had worked diligently for a promotion to the next level, and after being told that I was not aggressive enough or not experienced enough, I went above and beyond to show those claims to be untrue. I would show up unscheduled and unpaid to view rehearsals and tapings, soaking up everything there was to know about those productions. The next time positions were available I would apply again.

I would state my qualifications and my accomplishments when interviewed. Contract rules said I had to be interviewed if I applied, and each available job had to be posted. Then the person interviewing me made a big mistake. He told me that as long as he was in charge I would never get another promotion, specifically to the position of associate director. He said I should be satisfied that I was already getting frequent upgrades to that job status on a temporary basis.

But if I didn't get an official upgrade with a permanent title change, the operations managers could stop the upgrades whenever they felt like it and penalize me in the pocket where it mattered most. They often did. An upgrade to a higher category would guarantee a higher pay scale as long as I remained in that position. Blocked on the conventional path, I took the next step available to me, arbitration.

Because I realized that I was being stymied, whenever someone of note complimented me on doing a great job, I made it a point to ask, "Would you be comfortable putting that compliment in writing?" If the person did, I added that letter to a file of which decision-makers were unaware. We went to arbitration, and I won a resounding victory.

Prayer was essential before I took action and throughout the process. David defeated Goliath and the Philistines, who had menaced Israel and Saul's army for forty days. I also faced a giant that had to be defeated. Religion and race do not guarantee sanctity, because countless numbers of God's chosen people were misled by greed, hate, the lust for power, and other maladies. Though they were heirs to father Abraham, they neither did what was right nor offered true worship as they should have. Jesus warned that if those claiming kinship to Abraham did not serve the Lord in true form and spirit, they would be lost. He said the rocks would cry out to Him in the absence of their worship.

Strides in Hope and in Conflict

After the breakup with my second wife, I made progress in areas other than my career. I took these developments as a sign that I had not been completely one-dimensional in my choices and in my efforts. I filed immigration papers for my family in Jamaica and supplied the funds necessary to grant my older brother a permanent resident visa to the United States. He chose to bring his wife first and to have his children follow them after they could afford to support them. I filed papers for my mother and other siblings, but Mom remained in Jamaica a bit longer to care for my brother's children and until my two youngest siblings graduated from high school. She also wanted to settle some land issues. About a year after my brother's arrival, his children joined him. My mother and my siblings followed two years later.

During those years, work was arduous and demanding, so I needed an outlet to fight stress and frustration. I prayed constantly, but I also partied at clubs and friends' houses and dated quite frequently. Eventually I met a young lady who within a few years became my wife and bore me a son. I purchased a two-family brick home that I planned to share with my family from Jamaica. My relatives lived with us for about a year, but eventually all went their separate ways. I had hoped to combine our resources to acquire more real estate and to secure each person's future, but they were not interested and didn't understand the plan. They could not live together without conflict, and that troubled me greatly. I had conceded that the idea was unachievable.

Although I let go of the idea, I did not let go of my family. We were within minutes of each other's residences. My new wife had siblings in the United States, but her parents and the remainder of her siblings lived in Jamaica. Her mother and her sisters visited with us, and on our vacations to Jamaica we visited and stayed with them. We would make their home our base, fan out to other places on the island, and return there before coming back to the United States. With this arrangement, it became quite easy for others to have access to me and to my personal effects, and soon I returned to the position I had occupied in my father's house. This time an entirely different person or persons were violating me.

It has been hard to revisit certain events in my life. Some that I thought I had dealt with thoroughly were clearly not buried deep enough. The pain was just below the surface. When I told the story of my flower's mental breakdown, I was overcome with tears. I had not cried over the situation at the time it happened or when I heard that she had passed away. I had to be strong because too many people depended on me. But on the day I journeyed back, I sat at my desk and wept. Telling the story of my communications job and the arbitration produced a knot in my stomach.

I was given visions while I was with my new wife and after we separated and were going through a protracted divorce proceeding, blame could be appropriated in either direction. I have taken the blame in this relationship where it is legitimate and have not assigned it where it is undeserved.

One of my wife's sisters came to spend a vacation with us in our home, and the night before she flew back to Jamaica, packing the suitcases to hold all of her newly acquired stuff became an issue. My wife told her younger sister she did not know how to pack properly and threw everything out of the suitcases to be repacked. During the repacking, my wife found one piece after another of my personal belongings. She asked, “What are you doing with this stuff in your suitcase?” Her sister replied, “Oh, I washed some dirty clothes, and I must have picked these things up by mistake from the laundry.” That was a lie!

My wife removed the items. I don’t know whether her sister reclaimed them before leaving, but I do know that the same thing happened again without anyone being caught. There was a sinister plan to use those articles to do sinful deeds. Throughout our relationship, my wife’s relatives were always in my home and had access to me. By the time I had caught on to what was happening, my nights had become restless. In my dreams I was always fighting off snakes, alligators, scorpions, and lizards or being chased by dogs trying to tear me apart. But I always dreamed that I was flying. If you are flying in your dreams, this indicates that God has made a way of escape for you and that you are above the forces seeking to destroy you.

There were also times when I felt a presence pressing down on me and attempting to keep me from waking or from getting out of my bed. I told my wife about these occurrences, and she became very concerned. She told me that she had wondered whether her mother practiced witchcraft or was involved in it. As a child and as a young woman she had heard her mother and another woman arguing over a relationship and about accusations of witchcraft.

When you love someone, whether husband, wife, or child, be careful that you do not approve of or join them in acts that can wreak havoc in your life or the lives of others. Think this over carefully because you may never be able to escape the effects of some acts after the die has been cast.

In many places, if you consent to take someone to a place where a crime occurs or if you leave a door open to a criminal, you will be judged just as guilty as the person committing the crime and sentenced to the applicable punishment. Family members can bend your will, especially when they are completely convinced that you are living the good life and don't want them to enjoy the same things. They can play on your conscience and cause you to lose the trust and even the love of others to whom you should be committed.

When I realized what was happening to me in this marriage and saw that my wife had left the door open to someone who had come to rob, steal, and destroy, I became a judge, pronounced sentence, and carried out the punishment. I told myself I would not resort to an eye for an eye and would not get my hands dirty. Instead, I soiled my entire body and my pages in the Book of Life by retaliating with infidelity. I went out with other women to get even.

Much earlier, I had visited a business to arrange professional services and was greeted and helped by an assistant to the owner. We felt an immediate attraction, but I noted that I was happily married and I did not pursue that avenue. However, after discovering what was happening in my marriage, I returned and took advantage of that attraction. I went back on my declaration that I was happily married and would not go down the road of temptation. I surrendered to hurt, and now I regret it.

Only afterward did I realize that sin is sin and that I was just as accountable to God for what I did as my wife was for what she allowed. Yes, on her watch I got broadsided. But if we get hurt by others, we ought to forgive rather than to seek revenge. We should leave our hurts to God, or if the law provides an avenue for justice, we can seek that. Vengeance is mine, says the Lord.

Amid all this chaos on the job and at home, most people did not know there was a problem since I was a quiet, reserved person who did not broadcast my business all over. When it finally came out that we would be separating, this was a shock to many who saw us as a loving and successful couple suited to be together for a long time. After the breakup, however, some said they never thought ours was a good match.

Nineteen eighty-five was a year of turmoil but also a year of great enlightenment. I felt as though I was carrying a weight heavier than

I had ever borne, and I told my favorite cousin that I felt I was losing my mind. My wife and I were planning to vacation in Jamaica, and I was speaking to my cousin there about our trip. She told me to keep praying and said my relatives would keep me in their prayers. My cousin also advised me to spend time with my grandma and grandpa because they had a friend, a man of God and a powerful spiritual healer, I needed to see.

We got to Jamaica and used my wife's family home in Kingston as our base. From there we hooked up with her friends and went all over the island. When we arrived I was given a bag of weed, Jamaican sensimilla, touted as being the best. I had smoked sensimilla many times, but now I set it aside. I had no immediate desire to say, "Hooray! I'm on vacation, and I'm going to get messed up on this weed." I did not roll a joint, or a spliff as Jamaicans call it, until the next day. And after I rolled the spliff I set it aside and did not smoke it. Our friends had weed, and they also had connections in many places where we were hanging out—from Kingston all the way down to Negril. I left the weed at the house unsmoked.

After about two weeks of hanging out and having fun, we made plans to visit my grandparents at my father's birthplace. My mother's parents had died several years earlier, so only my father's parents remained. My wife and I and our son got into our rented car, picked up my cousin along the way, and went to the country to see my grandparents. We arrived, hugged and kissed, chatted about relatives, and passed on some gifts. Then my grandfather left to get the man of God. They arrived and my grandfather introduced the man, who asked that some chairs be set under a tree a short distance from the veranda. He then asked for a basin of clean water, and when it was brought out, he asked me to wash my face and my hands. He washed his face and his hands and prayed.

He looked at me but asked no questions, silently probing the depths of my life. He began with me as a young boy, telling me things that had happened twenty years before. He told me about the accident that hurt others rather than me when I was departing

Jamaica at fifteen. This event was planned, he confirmed. Then he discussed my father's house and how my personal belongings had been brought to Jamaica and were buried in a graveyard. He correctly named all of the players in each event and all of the items that were taken, noting how this affected me. He spoke about my flower and then about my job and the people at the communications company. Then he explained that my mother, my brothers, and my sister, whom I brought up from Jamaica, were part of a circle and that I was the one from whom help emanated. The Enemy had tied up all those in the circle, and that was why my plans for them did not come to fruition.

Next he told me that it was through God's intervention that I did not smoke that weed. The Lord had saved me from devastation, because if I had smoked it, I would have become totally mad. The sensimilla had been taken to a person who practiced witchcraft and had been fixed specially for me. He confirmed my suspicions about who was causing my woes and said he would do something for me before I returned to Kingston. We were going down to the river to have a swim, so he told me he would meet me there after gathering some local plants. But before he departed he declared, "In three days God is going to show you a sign."

I played with my son in the water, jumped off of rocks into the deep, and swam all over. I soaped up and bathed before getting out. We had been in the water for about twenty minutes when I saw the gentleman approaching. "Are you finished?" he asked, and I replied yes. He had a quiet aura. Though he was there in the flesh, he seemed far away in the spirit as he motioned to me to come to the river's edge. He gave me some leaves and told me to stand in the middle of the river, to pray to God, and to ask for whatever I wanted as I washed myself from the crown of my head to the soles of my feet with those leaves. I did that and then came out and got dressed. He told me not to worry and to keep praying.

He also told me that someone was given the duty of spying on me and bringing back reports of everything I did. This person was not there that day but had been accompanying us everywhere we had gone before. He had taken vacation time because he said he did not wish to miss out on all of the fun of having us in Jamaica, but his chief task was to keep watch. He was with us on our next journey to the country because I had arranged a family reunion with food, drinks, music, and games by the river.

Since we had been traveling so much, we stayed put at the home base in Kingston for the next few days before heading out of town again. We visited locally, meeting my wife's old school friends and former neighbors, but I planned a solo trip to my cousin's house on the third day. I got up early, telling everyone I wanted some time by myself to catch up with my cousin. My wife's relatives tried to convince me that the trip was not safe. I had not lived in Jamaica for many years, they said, and could be easily spotted by robbers as a target. I would be driving a rented car, which would stand out. I said I did not care. I drove off and spent most of the day with my cousin and her family.

This was a special day even though I did not dwell on the declaration that the man of God had given me. It had faded into the recesses of my mind. As I sat on the veranda of my cousin's home, I told her that I wanted something cold to drink. "You are not a stranger," she said, "so go get it from the fridge." I walked through the front sitting room into the dining room, which led into the kitchen, and above the door ledge hung a wooden sign that read: "God Is Love." As I caught sight of this sign, I felt the glory of God come down from heaven and embrace me. I felt an indescribable love, warmth, and peace. I stood there for a while until my cousin called out and asked if I saw the cold drinks. I told her I was looking at something and soon went into the kitchen and got a soda.

Returning to the veranda, I told her what had just happened, and she reminded me of what the man of God had prophesied. We then talked about how thankful the family had been to have him as a friend since he had helped us to work through so many challenges. This was the first of three occasions when God used an inanimate object to communicate with me. The second happened in 1988, and the third came in December of 2014 in a doctor's office in central Florida. I will discuss those encounters later.

Arriving at work the day after our return home, I immediately realized there was a problem awaiting me. Before going on vacation, I had taken a few sick days. I had gone to my doctor because a chronic sinusitis condition had flared up and then had gone on my vacation, which had been approved much earlier. I was now being told that I had taken more than my allotted vacation time since my sick days ran straight into my vacation. Department managers said I should have cut my vacation short to make up for the sick

time I took. They said I had extended my vacation by adding days when I was not actually sick. I challenged their arguments with doctor's notes from America and Jamaica, and they had to drop the issue.

I'm convinced senior managers were attempting to strike back at me for winning my arbitration claim of discrimination against them. They signed a legal document pledging not to do that. My longtime manager was moved out of his office and his position, which was given to a black female. She was double insurance since she qualified as a minority on two fronts. I believe she was given wide authority in hopes that I would quit, but the tactic did not work. I accepted every yoyo shift and every schedule denial with grace, and even when I was angry I did not lash out at anyone.

I gave managers no grounds to fire me. They were looking for ways to justify doing that. It was a bad feeling to have someone who sued them and won in their faces every day. I imagine every time they saw me they were reminded that I beat them despite their best attempt to defeat me. Work was quite awkward at times but I stuck it out. A friend who was a middle manager in another department had advised me not to bring the discrimination case because even if I won, I would become a target at the company. But I had made my choice and was living with it.

After my buddy had been moved out of his position, he called me and asked me to come to his new office. He had been my manager for a long time and was familiar with my work record and my ethics. We first talked about his new office and his new job and about how things were changing at the company. I felt the hurt in his voice and saw it in his eyes. He had risen from the bottom ranks and had dedicated many years and long hours to the company. He always had good words for the organization, but the new management decision bothered him.

He then told me what was on his mind, but he spoke in a parable, advising me to take any opportunity I could get outside of the company because, "The shuffling that happened was the best-laid plans of mice and men." He recommended another local company where I would have more opportunities to hone my skills and might become a director. I listened but I knew that someone there held a hammer and would block any move even if I followed my friend's advice. I was at a good level already, and it was either do or die trying. I was going to stay.

I had been getting bad feelings whenever I saw news stories about unemployment around the nation. I had never had this eerie, unnatural feeling in my many years in the news business. This feeling portended what loomed in the future, and that is why it affected me so much. One night I went to bed and the Lord God showed me what was to come. In that vision I was taken above my home. On my left was an angel in bright white splendor, and on my right was another angel with the same bright aura. Their large outstretched wings were bearing me up. My house was completely engulfed in flames, which shot up thirty feet or more above the roof. We were just above these flames, but they did not burn us. No words were spoken, but the message came to me through the Holy Spirit that I would face the fiercest fires of my life but would not be destroyed.

I kept having those eerie feelings regarding unemployment, and I was shown visions in which a medical team was conducting experiments on me. These creatures wore lab coats, but their heads and faces were covered. I could not tell if they were humans or aliens, and I did not share these visions with anyone, because they seemed to come from a B-movie script. I didn't have a history of illness and had not undergone surgery in some high-tech operating room. I had had only minor surgery in an office setting.

I was being shown places where I had not yet been, and when I found myself there physically, I told myself, *I've been here before.* While all of this was going on, I was becoming agitated about living in such a deceptive environment. I wanted to stay away from home more than I wanted to be there. I would sleep about five or six hours for a day or two, but I often could not sleep more than three or four hours. It was indeed a challenge to sleep peacefully in my house.

When I came back from Jamaica, I decided that I didn't want to have relatives occupy my basement, which was now finished. Someone was trying to migrate to America and had asked if we would allow her to live there. I had previously said yes. I also decided to stop smoking weed and never to accept it from anyone. I also resolved to be more selective about what I ate and about the people from whom I accepted food. After my wife returned from Jamaica, I had a heart-to-heart talk with her about how I felt. We had problems in our marriage, but I loved her and had made sure that she had everything. I did not exclude her family but had received a slap in the face in return. I told her she had to decide whether she was going to stand by me all the way and forsake all who would do me harm for their gain.

I had been blessed with the gift of discernment, so I saw things as they were and not just as people wanted me to see them. Since the night I was taken up by the angels, my gift had been strengthened. I was upgraded at work and was being paid as an associate director since the arbitration, but I had not been given an official promotion to the title. I was assigned to a morning program and sometimes worked in the afternoons into the nights. I was given these assignments to keep me from the mainstream and to deny me a platform to excel as I did before. This would ensure that I would not amass any more awards or commendation letters that I could use against management.

After my arbitration, I had the opportunity to meet the first black director for my division. We talked about the issues at the company, about how they affected me and others, and about the politics at hand. He promised me that if I worked for him on any show and did a great job, he would stand by me and make sure that I got my just due. I did not want to work any more odd shifts, but I wanted to make sure that this brother shined like no one the company had seen before. I didn't want to give anyone the opportunity to claim that blacks didn't have the intelligence or the discipline to handle the job or to excel at it.

The usual line since passage of the Equal Employment Opportunity Act was, "We could not find a candidate qualified enough to fill the position." So I worked on the first show to which this man was assigned and gave him my all. When he got his second show, I helped since I had worked on it previously. I went back with the desire to help him in any way I could to make sure he was just as excellent there. He stood by me, and I'm forever grateful to him.

So from 1985 into '86 I was still doing one show's afternoon pre-production for the next day's broadcast and many times staying over to do the live broadcast in the morning. I finally got an official promotion, but as fate would have it, about six months later I was lumped into a company-wide layoff as the person with the least seniority now that I had been promoted. I remembered the words of my former manager about "the best-laid plans of mice and men." The plan had been cloaked in secrecy with many moving parts, but God had already taken care of me. The pension plan with my bargaining unit required ten years of service and contributions to be vested, and I had made my ten years between the time I was hired as a program production assistant and the time of my layoff. I was secure.

A Season of Ousting and Casting Off

This was an era of buyouts, mergers, and hostile takeovers. Cuts to personnel were being made, and so this was the perfect opportunity for those targeting me. They could throw me out under the guise of an above-board move. I was given a severance package, but I decided to contact my bargaining unit because I knew what had taken place and I wanted to present a swift challenge.

It was contract bargaining time, and talks were not going well. Management was threatening a lockout of the bargaining unit's members if they would not bend on givebacks. People will go to great lengths to hurt one another, but when the fire grows most intense we are being prepared for something special.

I wanted to have the bargaining-unit attorney who defended me the first time defend me again, but that was not to be, because she was deemed unsuitable for this case. I was at the mercy of the legal defense provided, and my contract said I had to attempt arbitration before I could go to court. I was told I would have the best person for the job defending me.

I contacted my former attorney and asked why she could not defend me but did not tell her what I had heard from others. She told me she had no control over what was going on, but as I pressed further, she said that if she told me anything about what was happening, she could lose her license to practice law since there was a confidentiality issue with her employer. She sympathized with me, and I understood that she had to protect her livelihood, especially if the loss would be a great one. Disbarment from practicing law is no small matter.

I pursued the challenge to be reinstated in my position and or to be compensated generously if I was not reinstated. But the plan had been hatched long before, and everything that took place was a farce and a subterfuge. The company presented no credible evidence. People who had not even worked with me gave hearsay testimony and repeated fabrications prepared by management to show that others were more qualified to be kept on instead of me. In the end the arbitrator found that there was no substantive evidence against me and that the company had incorrectly laid me off, but due to the firm's financial problems, evident in layoffs documented in news reports, she was unable to award me financial compensation and could not order me to be reinstated since that would cause further hardship to the company. What about me? Didn't I deserve a crumb from the table?

What a decision! I went in knowing that an arbitrator's decision was final even if the arbitrator made a mistake in the ruling or misapplied the law. My goose was thoroughly cooked. Everyone attached to the case disappeared when the ruling was coming down, and I had to hound every available person for ten days to find out whether a ruling had been made and what it was. Ten full days of response time was lost because no one contacted me by mail, by telephone, or by any other means. My newly hired attorney and I had twenty days to mount a challenge to this erroneous decision.

My law firm and I fought all the way from the lower courts to the Supreme Court, lodging a complaint with the Equal Employment Opportunity Commission, but were rebuffed on all fronts since an arbitrator's decision stands forever. The Supreme Court rejected my case, unwilling to reverse the law or even to modify it to suit an unknown man fighting a large corporation. My former employer vigorously battled me, using its large resources and multiple lawyers. It probably would have been much cheaper to compensate me fairly than to have used up so much of its time and money, but the company wanted to win at any cost.

At the time, I did not understand that God's plan for me at the company had been accomplished. I did not need to go back or to fight for anything else, but I did not understand that then. I had accomplished my mission by working at the company and by being part of the same program I had seen on that special day in1969. Gaining security with the pension plan was another mission accomplished. But I felt there was much more to be accomplished that had been wrestled away from me, and I was hurt and angry about it. That is why I continued to fight after the layoff when I should have walked away, letting God be the final arbiter. I had to drop the case in the end, and He will be that final arbiter.

My premonition about losing my job and my career had come true, and though I felt I was going to lose my mind, God prevented that from happening. Next my marriage would unravel and come to an end to free me from that alliance. As I have noted, from 2005 to 2014 I had fourteen surgeries. I have come to realize that they were revealed in those visions in which aliens seemed to have taken me aboard a spaceship for medical experiments. To top it off, I had to use my retirement benefits early when my kidneys failed. I had to declare early retirement because of compound medical issues. I was fully vested.

Searching for the Elusive Ladder

At age thirty-five I was fighting a spiritual battle, a labor and employment battle, a divorce battle, and a battle to protect and to secure my two children. Jamaicans have a saying that if you can't catch someone, you catch his shirt. This recalls the story of Joseph, the son of Jacob, who was sold into slavery. When Joseph was in Potiphar's house in Egypt and escaping from the amorous desires of Potiphar's wife, she caught hold of his outer garment and used it to frame him and to inflict undeserved punishment on him (Genesis 39).

One day the mother of the best friend of my former wife took me aside and asked if what she had been hearing about our situation was true. I told her it was. She asked, "Are you sure?" She told me she knew a very good man who was a spiritualist and if indeed what she had been hearing was true, he would tell her. She said she had two sons and would not be pleased if someone was doing to them what she had heard was happening to me. She asked if I would be willing to go with her to meet the spiritualist, and I agreed. We made the arrangement for the next week when she was off from work. We met early in the morning to do this so that she could keep her other appointments during the day.

I picked her up in my car and she gave me directions to the gentleman's house. We went in and I was introduced. They made small talk, and then it was on to business. He confirmed to her what was happening and what had happened. Now she was bewildered because as she said to me, "You have been a good man to her and her family. She is my daughter's good friend and you have become my friend, and this is not a good situation." What would you do in a situation like this? How would you handle your friendship and your affiliations?

My finances were greatly strained, so I had sold my home, rented an apartment, and tried to settle with my wife, but the battle dragged on for many years. At one point I hoped it was ending. I placed my belongings in storage, gave up the apartment, and began staying with a great friend whose boy is my godson. I planned to relocate to California for a fresh start since an exploratory trip to Atlanta had not netted me any prospects. Every professional inquiry had to go back to my former employer since I had worked there for the past twelve years.

There was an interesting development after I returned from Atlanta. With no solid prospects for a job, I came home and checked my answering machine for messages. There were no recorded messages, but there was indeed a message. I had a special recorded message that said who I was, thanked callers, apologized for being unable to take their calls, and asked that they leave a message so I could return their calls as soon as possible. That message was erased, and in its place was a recording that said, "This message to pray is from the Spirit."

I called my friend and asked her to listen to the message. I asked her if she had recorded it, but she said no. She was scared when she heard it and shook with fear. I comforted her and told her not to be afraid. The voice had a certain tonality and pitch as if a preacher had spoken those words. This message had me deep in submission and wonder, but I knew who had sent it. I just had to rule out any other possibility since I was not the only one occupying the apartment and others had access to the answering machine. This was the second time that God had communicated with me through an inanimate object.

The divorce proceedings were delayed so many times that I had to put off going to California. I wound up staying too long at my friend's apartment, exhausted all of my sources of cash, and had to accept an offer to stay at the apartment my mother, my sister, and my brother occupied. I took a job I thought I was going to do part time but was convinced to do it full time. I needed the little money it paid, but it was not the money that persuaded me; it was the will of God. The job was with a foundation that operated group homes. As a supervisor, I had to take a course to be certified as a life skills professional, a course to defuse or to control physical situations, and a course to be certified to dispense medications. The classes were at a psychiatric center where a great many mentally challenged people were being housed and cared for. This was the population I would work with at the group home.

At my first glimpse of these people I was terrified and unsure if I could do this job, but God had prepared the way. I began work as the supervisor of a group home with more than twenty men, ranging from their late teens to their seventies, and a staff that included a psychologist, a social worker, a manager, an assistant manager, a nurse, a cook, and maintenance workers. States were requiring that large warehouse mental facilities be closed and that the residents be integrated into society.

That was our goal at the group home, a new facility with veteran specialists and newly trained ones like me. The challenge was great, but I wound up staying with that job for more than three years. I managed staff and a budget, administered medications, and even gave baths, helping residents reach goals and teaching life skills. The work was sometimes frustrating in the beginning, but God wanted me to see how fortunate I had been despite what I had endured. He always let me know that He would take care of me because He loved me. Soon after I began the work, I became comfortable with the residents and was no longer afraid. I learned how to embrace a person who had made me feel squeamish. God's love allowed me to build the fruits of the Spirit. He was rebuilding me in His special way, and that way included love, joy, peace, patience, kindness, goodness, faithfulness, gentleness, and self-control. I was being rededicated in Christ Jesus.

I became quite comfortable about being seen in the company of the residents, and so I would take them all over the city and the county to events and restaurants. Sometimes people would tell me that they could never do what I was doing, but they thanked God that He had given me the patience to be caring and kind. On a few occasions people gave me money to treat residents to dinner, to lunch, or to ice cream. This made them feel part of society. This was one of the most rewarding spiritual training sessions I have ever had. The three years-plus was a lesson in love, compassion, forgiveness, patience, humility, and trust. This experience was not easy. I was punched in the jaw, kicked, spat on, and cursed out without mercy many times. On the other hand, I was recognized with awards for excellence in the field.

Even as I was helping these people, I was often barraged with racial slurs. It is sad how bias can attach itself to a person and take root. If this happens without correction, the bias keeps regenerating itself in that person even in his waning years. I could not help but feel sad for one repeat offender who used these slurs. He used this language to debase the minority staff and to declare that he was still a white man and that no such persons were going to tell him what to do and how to do it. We human beings waste precious time trying to establish our kingdoms here on earth when we should be preparing our souls to meet God. We wind up digging inescapable pits for ourselves. What are you doing with your life today?

It was now 1990 and my daughter was going off to college soon. Losing my job and my career had been a blessing in that I could spend time with my daughter at home and at the library, attend parent-teacher conferences, and help her academically. Previously

I had left that responsibility to her mother and her grandmother, and things had not gone well. My daughter had floundered in her middle school years and had not built on her academic roots, so I had to reestablish the core foundations in math, science, writing, and reading comprehension. She applied to eight colleges and was accepted at five. We narrowed down the number and made visits, did interviews with recruiters, administrators, and advisers, and then selected a college.

My daughter and I had built a bond that had been tested and had grown stronger. She was always with me on weekends and on holidays and usually all summer long when she was not living with me full time, so she was very much aware of what I was enduring, because she was going through it with me. We had an understanding that there was nothing we could not discuss, because I would always be in her corner regardless of the situation. The school we chose with the Lord's leading was a thousand miles away, but He had a surrogate mother in place, waiting for her arrival.

The good friend I had stayed with before I moved in with my mom and my family had had an opportunity to pray with a female evangelist on the telephone a few years before and passed on her number to me. I called this lady and we talked and prayed and immediately established a spiritual bond. In 2015, she told me that the first time we talked and prayed, she had learned that God had planted a ministry in me. This evangelist is a prophetess with a ministry and is so anointed that God has used her in a mighty way in my life, in my daughter's life, and in the lives of countless other people. I thank God for this person.

The evangelist introduced us to a friend who was a graduate of the college we had chosen. When we flew to her state, we first stopped off to spend the day with the evangelist and her family. Then we went on to meet her friend. She greeted us with open arms and said my daughter would be safe and welcomed in her home whenever she chose to come. My daughter had to live on campus her first two years but spent a lot of weekends at this woman's home and traveled with her. This loving lady had not had a daughter, only a son, and right away unofficially adopted my daughter.

My daughter's decision to attend school outside of our state was an attempt to escape the big city so she could be in a smaller setting and focus on her education. God knew her desires and the hills we had already climbed, so just as He did for the children of Israel wishing to escape Egypt, He opened the Red Sea before us and gave us safe passage on dry land. He made a way of escape and provided a refuge for my daughter. She and I agreed that I should go back to college, but I would postpone my return until she had finished her first year. This was absolutely necessary to make college financially feasible for both of us and so that I could help with her initial studies.

When I began the process of returning to school, I was still employed with the foundation that ran the group homes and still bunking with my family. My mother had convinced me to stay and to try to straighten out my issues instead of going somewhere else where I could fail completely. She was aware of all the obstacles I faced and didn't mind that we lived in a cramped situation as long as she knew I was okay. As we discussed life and the evil that continually sought to destroy me, she told me that I needed to seek a source of help because God's people are here on earth to assist Him. Since my vision of the angels taking me above my home away from the fire below, the demonic assault had intensified. I never argued with my mother but always told her that God would work out all my problems. A mother always worries about her child regardless of how old that child is.

Climbing the Ladder of Hope Again

When I began researching colleges and universities I looked for academic relevance with affordability, so I was basically limiting myself to lower-end schools. I submitted an application to a college and was accepted, but the Spirit of the Lord said, *No, not that one. Keep looking.* He rejected every school after that until I was led to a top private university. I questioned God about how I would pay for my education there, and He reassured me that I should enroll and stop worrying. I requested the necessary enrollment packet and went forward. On the evening of the entrance exams, most youngsters finished quickly and turned in their papers. I was left with about five other persons in the large auditorium.

I took time to go over my exam after I had completed it, so when I turned it in, the proctor asked if everything was okay. I said yes. She said she had been worried that I would not finish since only about thirty minutes were left on the clock. I told her I was making sure I used the time wisely, and she wished me luck in parting. When I received my acceptance letter, it came with a few scholarship offers, both academic and need-based. God worked things out so that in all four years I received scholarships, cutting my costs in half. I had to borrow money through student loans, but in four years I left with an associate's degree in marketing and a bachelor's degree in organizational management and in communications. I was often on the honor roll and the dean's list.

My daughter and I graduated in 1995. I had gone through a graduation before, but because of my multiple degrees, this was the big one for me. My daughter's pace was a bit slower than mine, but though we graduated separately we still did it together. I had returned to college for my benefit but also to motivate my daughter since she had told me just before my layoff that she did not want to go to college. All the expenses were my responsibility. I had to pay off all of our debts to graduate. I did this, graduated in early May, and was flat broke. I had no idea where I would find the cash to travel a thousand miles to my daughter's graduation, but God knew.

The last time I had seen or heard from my stepbrother was sometime in 1986, and out of the blue he called me, asked how I was doing, and said he needed to see me later that day. I said I would be home, and he came by within two hours. He apologized that he had taken so long to repay a loan that I had made to him twenty years ago. Then he peeled off a number of crisp hundred-dollar bills and said, "I think this will cover the balance." I said it would. He told me how badly his conscience had bothered him over the years, knowing he had not repaid the money, and I told him not to feel bad because I had not thought about the loan at all. I had forgotten about it, so this repayment was right on time.

We talked for a while, and he said good-bye and left. Isn't God great? He knew exactly what I needed, and He provided it. I used the money to rent a full-size car that transported four adults and one small child to and from my daughter's graduation with gas and tolls paid. I also paid for a hotel rental. The other occupants prepared and packed food, drinks, and snacks and contributed funds toward a celebration with friends of the graduate before we returned home. God is great all the time and not just when we need Him.

God had told my stepbrother to contact me and to provide what I needed. I don't know if he recognized God's voice, because I have not discussed this event with him, but I will. That he was able to pay me that five hundred dollars is also a miracle. God will cause gifts to be moved out of closed fists into hands that will release those gifts.

There is a long story behind all of this, but suffice it to say that my stepbrother had received a great amount of money to manage when his mother, my former stepmother, became very ill and couldn't handle personal or business affairs. My father had sold a home and had split the proceeds in two, minus a small amount for repairs and improvement before listing.

My father had adopted a hard line toward me for many reasons, but the most recent at that time was that he mistakenly believed I was not someone he should hold dear. He sided with my former wife because she had borne a son who would continue the family name. Men of an older generation, such as my dad, often equated worth and respect with the ability to bear a son.

My former wife made him feel good whenever he came over by preparing his favorite Jamaican specialties, which he was not getting at home from his new wife. My daughter was continually appalled at the way my father treated me, but I always told her not to worry, because he had told me from an early age that everyone had to make his own way. I told her that whatever my dad had did not belong to me and that it was his prerogative to decide what to do with it.

The issue was not about the money but about acknowledging me as he should have done. From the time I was a newborn, he gave me token recognition, but deep within he was unwilling to fully embrace me. When I was employed at a major company, he was proud to a point, but he got the story twisted. I think in his mind, I had allowed myself to lose my job, had sold my house and walked away from my marriage without good reason, and had wasted my money and become worthless. Nothing else mattered, whether it was the adversity I faced on the job or at home or whether I had used my money to fight for my career, to support my children, or to pay for education. What mattered to him was that I had no money, no house, and no car because I had sold it, so whatever I was doing had no value.

This is a summation of my relationship with my father, but God can change anyone's heart. When I came to Florida we had issues and my dad was unkind, but after I got sick and lost my kidneys and was near death, his attitude changed. He realized I was his only child. He had not heard from his stepchildren, even the ones he had shown so much love. He realized I was his son, and since then we have had a kind and peaceful relationship. He supported my efforts in my first ministry and cheered when God made me a pastor. He is always at the ministry and helps out wherever and whenever he can. My dad is very much a part of my family and is a friend to my wife and to all our children and grandchildren.

God is more than able to turn any situation around. If you listen and remain where He wants you to be, the change will come pouring down like fresh oil. I never cussed out my dad or banished him from my life, but sometimes I kept my distance when the hurt was fresh and tried again later. Looking back, I was wrong to fight him when he unfairly disciplined me. In doing this, I dishonored him in God's eyes. It was not my place to take corrective action against him. It was God's responsibility. We ought to honor our mothers and our fathers in all things so that we will have long, God-blessed lives. Today I'm at peace with my dad, and I think that he is at peace with me.

My biological mother left us in the fall of 1991 after I had begun to make great strides to regain my footing. Just before she passed, she spoke of things I had not known about as well as some I had. She reminded me about a bank account she had as well as a will she had drawn up many years before. She also reminded me about a conversation we had long ago in which I had told her not to worry about me, because I had carved out my own life and would always be able to take care of myself. She told me things were a lot different now, and I should not continue to think that way but accept what was in the will.

A few days before she passed she entered my bedroom after taking a bath and asked me to put some lotion on her bare back because she had an itch and could not reach it. I had not done anything like that for my mother since I was a child, but she was not naked; only her back was exposed. I felt a bit awkward, but nevertheless as a dutiful and loving son I did as she asked. After she fell ill, I recognized that these were all signs that she would soon leave us.

The night before she fell ill, I had a vision of a running stream, and when I viewed the portion just across from me, I saw what looked like an oil slick on the surface. The slick drifted downstream and was gone. When I woke up and pondered the vision, I saw it as a special one. But what did it mean? My mother and I spent the day together. We watched television in the morning, and then I prepared for an exam in my first evening class. We said good-bye when I went off to school in the late afternoon. During the exam I felt something was not quite right, but I did not know exactly what, so as soon as I finished the exam I left school, skipping my second class. I rushed home and there in front of our building was an emergency ambulance. I ran upstairs, opened the door, and found the EMTs working on my mother in the middle of the living room. They placed her on a gurney and raced to the hospital. She had suffered a massive stroke and was placed on a breathing machine. There was swelling on the brain stem, and I knew this was the end.

I contacted my prayer partner by telephone and we prayed, but we knew that her time had come. My brothers and sister wanted to keep my mother on the breathing machine, but I knew she had left us, so I decided against it. On the fourth day after her stroke, she was pronounced dead by the physicians. We took time off and gave her services in America and in Jamaica where she was buried. She was lost to the physical world, but she had a strong disposition, and later when I was hurt by a decision my siblings made and by their manner of communication, her spirit came through more than once asking me to forgive them and to give them another chance. I took her advice after her second spiritual communication.

When we were traveling to Jamaica to bury my mother, someone who knew me and my former wife asked if I was going on a vacation, and I said, "No, to bury my mother." She asked when my mother had died, and I told her the date. She was puzzled. "So your mother died on the same day that your wife's mother died?" she asked. I responded that I did not know that her mother died, and she said, "Yes; she died." Why is this important? Just before my mother died, I had a dream in which a voice spoke of Luke 16:19. I looked up the verse. It is about Lazarus and the rich man. Just as the person on the airplane told me the news about that other death, this verse came to mind.

A few years before, my prayer partner and friend, the evangelist and prophetess, had conveyed a special message from God to me. While she was praying, the Lord God told her to say to me, "Do not lose focus, for the evil within her will roll up like a ball in her belly and she shall die." Sometimes suffering must continue for a while, but when will we be released from our enemies? We do not know, but God does. Whether our enemies are dead or alive, we ought to keep praying and to keep trusting in God while we push forward. During that same time of prophecy, the Spirit of God also directed the evangelist to have me make Proverbs 3 my guide and my companion. I did, and this chapter of Scripture keeps me grounded and free even today.

I have not spoken much about attending church, but I had been doing this all along. I used to attend a Catholic church with my former wife, because she was Catholic. I had my fill of the routine after some years, so we moved on. In 1986 I attended a mega church that had a fantastic worship and praise, and I was truly arrested by the Holy Spirit. I did not know exactly what was happening at the time, and I tried to keep control of the situation by refusing to let myself go. I did not go up to the altar call since I was determined not to allow anyone to lay hands on me. I stayed in my seat while others I came with went down to the altar, but I wept, repented, and solidified my hope and my desire to serve. I have learned that even when the Holy Spirit is moving, not everyone who is laying on hands should be doing so.

In 1987 I visited two ministries and had an opportunity to talk to an old friend, who invited me to home meetings she was attending. When I checked them out, I discovered that they involved Buddhist meditation and chanting. I was not down with that, and after attending a service at the temple to experience it, I decided I had had enough. I knew the mantras and the chants, but at the temple when we were asked to profess that Buddha was the true god, I faked a yawn and covered my mouth. After I stopped attending, the leader of the home meetings got a hold of my telephone number and would not stop calling me and inviting me to return. I did not continue attending, because I knew that Jesus Christ was the head of my life. I was not about to trade him off.

In the following years, leading up to 1995, I visited with new ministries and kept having visions of baptisms. I did not see myself, but I saw other people being baptized. In the summer in 1995 my younger brother shared with me his plan to be baptized in his church, and I thought I was in the right frame of mind to do the same. I asked him to find out how I might be baptized at this church. He asked and church leaders said I had to take the preparation class, attend services, and obtain the items of clothing needed, so I did just that. I got baptized in the Atlantic Ocean, and when I was submerged and brought up, the pastor held a large wooden cross above me. That was the first thing I saw when I emerged from the lowering, and even now the cross is still before me.

I stayed in that ministry as a courtesy for four or five months, never becoming a member. I moved on when felt led to do so. The next two ministries I attended offered similar experiences. Each one provided something that God wanted to teach me, and when it was time to move on He nudged me and I did. In 1996 I met a dear friend who is now a bishop in a new ministry. She had not been ordained at the time, but she had a charisma and a joy in worship that drew everyone to her. When she was called to institute her own ministry, I would visit and worship with her in addition to attending the main ministry to which God directed me.

I had asked God to show me where He wanted me to be. Toward the end of 1997, He directed me to Bethany Baptist ministry. I was a member of that ministry until I left the Northeast United States. In all of those ministries were nuggets of wisdom that God chose, teaching me what to do and what not to do as He elevated me. All of those situations were unique in their own way. In this last ministry the senior pastor was regarded as a consummate preacher. His daddy and granddaddy were also preachers. It turned out that a portion of his life was a model of my life to come. While I was there, he had a kidney transplant and returned to the pulpit, and to God be the glory. I did not know that I was to suffer the same fate, but God is always giving us clues about every aspect of living.

THE LADDER'S MANY STEPS

I was trying to regain my footing as the fall semester began in 1993. The college was offering pre-calculus, so I enrolled in this class, but at the same time I kept an eye on the newspaper job listings. I wanted to continue working a full-time job while taking a full load of classes. There was a listing seeking marketing/sales representatives for an environmental conservation company. The ad mentioned salary plus commissions and I applied. After two interviews, I was told that I was among the final five for the third interview. The company was seeking to fill three slots.

On the eve of my third and final interview my barber cropped my hair closely and trimmed my facial hair, and I looked great. The next day I wore a newly dry-cleaned suit with pressed shirt and tie. As I began the interview, all was going well, but then disaster struck. I was sitting in a chair, posture right, clothes cleaned and pressed, face and hair immaculate. As I was answering a question about my experience and about why the company should hire me, I felt the chair collapse under me and thought I had fallen flat on my rear end onto the ground. In reality, I was still sitting upright, and everything else about my person was the same.

The moment I completed my sentence, the interviewer went way out to left field and was no longer talking about my strengths.

He told me that my beard looked scraggly. I asked if there was a company policy against employees having beards and said that if there was I could be clean shaven. He said it wasn't company policy to be clean shaven, but he began to end the interview. I thanked him for having considered me, and I made my exit from the office and the building.

So what happened? I had been spiritually attacked as I sat in that interview. Since I was constantly praying with God's covering, I was not controlled, but the spirit controlled the interviewer, who looked at my freshly shaved and manicured beard and called it scraggly. He was deflected by the intrusive spirit and then ended the interview, which would have gained me a job I was counting on. I needed a boost in my financial status to better meet my needs, but it was not to be at that company.

To add insult to injury, there was another incident. I had started my pre-calculus class, and a few days later I was about to take my first test of the semester. We were given the usual test booklets and a separate list of question. I wrote my name, the subject, and the class number on the booklet, but that was all I was able to do. Something came over me and I lost my memory completely. I tried to remember even the minutest fact or to solve the easiest of the problems, and I could not. I turned in the booklet and informed the professor that I had an issue and would be withdrawing from the course and would be submitting the necessary papers.

I shared my experience with another student who was quite friendly and who believed in the Scriptures and knew the evils we face on this earth. She gave me the name and the address of an adviser. When I arrived at the address, I found many people waiting, and it took hours to see this man. I almost left in frustration, considering all the other things I wanted to do, but because I always had reading materials with me, I read while waiting. I did schoolwork and finally I was called in to his office. There sat a small man dressed in white from head to toe. He wore what looked like a yarmulke on his head, but he wasn't Jewish. He motioned to me to sit down, and he asked my name and my date of birth. The man looked intently at me for a while and then laughed. "So you thought you didn't need anybody's help?" he said. Then he asked me if I saw all the people out in the waiting area, and I nodded yes. He said that there was much evil on this earth but that God had His people among us to help the suffering.

The man spoke to me about the kinds of people who sought help and said that he saw my financial situation and knew that I had suffered much. He said, "You need help right away or you will fail all of your classes. It was good that you withdrew from the one class so you did not lose that money, but the intent of the Enemy is that you will fail all of your classes." The man said that he saw I was trustworthy and that I would make a donation later, and he helped me. I missed making the dean's list that semester because I had withdrawn from that class, which was reported as an incomplete. I retook the class the following semester without issues and graduated from college with multiple degrees and with a decent grade point average. I always took full-load semesters and even helped my daughter a thousand miles away to write and to fine-tune her papers and to solve math problems. We both made it!

Just before graduation I lost the part-time sales and marketing job I had had for almost three years. I had many classes in addition to senior projects I had to finish within certain time periods, and I kept having to cancel shifts as well as falling short of sales quotas. I got unemployment insurance to tide me over while I looked for a job and a new career. Toward the end of the summer I saw an intriguing job posting in a newspaper but told my daughter to go on the interview since she had a science degree. She had the interview but was not offered a job.

The posting said that there would be two weeks of interviews and that hirees would be called back in three days. When my daughter was not called back, I went for an interview on the second-to-last day they were offered. The interviewer immediately told me, "I want to hire you, but don't leave because I want you to have two more interviews with my managers to see if we can finalize the hiring." I did as the interviewer asked and was hired. I would be given a date by telephone to report for training.

I was hired as a supervisor to work in a local office, but I trained in another state while the office was renovated. The travel was long and irksome, but that was where I was supposed to be. Before getting the job, I had a dream in which I was walking in this building's hallway near a cafeteria or a restaurant. The hallway had a décor that I recognized after about three or four days of work at the company. That feeling of déjà vu came upon me before I remembered the dream. When I saw that setting, I was convinced that God's hand had brought me to this place. The salary was half of what I was hoping for, but the benefits were great and the company was fairly young. I had certain expectations because of my financial situation and thought I needed much more to survive, but God knows best.

That first job out of college started me in an entirely new career in insurance management, and since this was my first foray into the field I had to take customer service classes and to gain telephone experience. I had to fully understand the products and the services offered by such companies. I later moved into account servicing, focusing on large groups. My pay rose with promotions, and though I later had to take a buyout package, I went on to work for a second such company.

When I decided to leave the Northeast United States at the urging of our Lord, I resigned from this job. It had become quite burdensome, and I did not regret leaving. In 2001 two days after the 9/11 attacks, I was standing on the street awaiting a bus when a woman asked if she could speak to me. She said she lived in Canada and was in the United States visiting a sick relative. She said God wanted her to deliver a message to me. I did not know her and she did not know me or anything about my past with the communications company, but she told me that God acknowledged my hurts and that He was not pleased with the treatment of minorities in America and would show His displeasure. She also said that the 9/11 attack was not the only disaster New York City would face and that the city would suffer a major flood. When Hurricane Sandy came up the East Coast, I recalled this prophecy. The storm brought devastation to all of the Northeast, not just to New York City.

After 9/11, my desire to live in the Northeast diminished. The job environment was perpetually tense, and I had grown tired of this atmosphere. The cutthroat culture of management versus union could not be changed. It was deeply embedded in the psyche of corporations and in many employees. Workplace stress often brought a spike in my blood pressure. My eyes would become blood red from the increase. Sometimes a situation must get dicey before you are convinced to clock out.

I relocated to south Florida, lived there for a short while, and then moved to my father's home in central Florida. God has a keen sense of humor, and I sense that He was providing a way to ensure that my father and I would be at peace with each other in the end. Before I moved into my father's house, I got a job at a mortgage company. I had done job searches, sent out résumés, and gotten a few interviews but didn't find work until about four months after moving to Florida. When I arrived for my interview at the mortgage company, a hundred or more dragonflies were dancing around my car. They stayed with me until I parked and exited the car. I found that quite unusual and saw it as a sign of something different ahead.

The interview went well and I was asked when I could start. I had nothing else to do, so I said the beginning of the following week would be fine. I was placed in the next training class. My intuition about the dragonflies was confirmed after I had moved to central Florida. The church that the Spirit of God had sent me to help build needed mortgage money and a person with financial knowhow. I thought I should have been hired for several jobs in the insurance field but wasn't. Then God provided a new opportunity. That's why I wound up as a mortgage qualifier despite the opposition of the woman who was then my mate. She thought I would be wasting my time and not getting the benefits that I merited given my qualifications. How could I even consider working for peanuts? We needed an immediate cash infusion and not the promise of future earnings. But God will place you where He can best use you to glorify Him. The test is not where you want to be or where someone else wants you to be but where He wants you to be.

You can find yourself in some sticky situations, though, even when God is directing your pathway, but rest assured that whatever situation you face, He will show you a way or will solve the problem Himself. So God placed me in my father's house, but as the situation soured, it was time to move to another house that He had willed for my life. He had prepared the woman whom He had in mind to be my wife. We got married and moved with her family into a rented house. She worked two jobs and we struggled financially. Every time I tried to work, I was stopped, and then sickness came upon me.

During my second illness I had no medical insurance. I was married but not on my wife's insurance policy because I had a job and was on the brink of a ninety-day qualifying period. However, I had to devote myself entirely to the ministry. After three weeks in intensive care, I emerged with a bill of $124,000. God took care of the bill, because I did not have that kind of money. The bill for my next hospitalization was $42,000, and God also took care of that one.

I was never a sickly person, so I had never been in such a precarious situation without insurance and unable to pay my bills. But my vision of God's angels holding me above my burning home was a clear message to rely on God and not on my own understanding. Proverbs 3 tells us to do just that and to believe that God can do all we hope for and more. In prophecies, I had been told many times that I would encounter losses but that God would restore everything many times over. I believed these prophecies and saw all of these setbacks as part of God's master plan.

My student loans were also piling up fees and interest since I had taken several deferments. I had graduated in 1995 and it was now 2005, so I began to think very hard about these rising costs. I had already paid $25,000 in interest, but it seemed as if I had paid nothing on the debt. After doing research to see whether I could get relief from the debt, I found guidelines telling me exactly how to do that.

The guidelines said that if I had end-stage renal disease and could provide three years of valid medical documentation, then my federal student loans could be invalidated. I had the disease, and for three years I submitted medical proof. At the end of the final year, I was awarded a total invalidation, rescinding any responsibility for a $103,000 debt.

The Lord God showed me His promise in His golden light in 2003 and again in 2014. The Scripture passages describing heaven and things associated with God tell us about His riches in glory and say that the streets are gold. People who have been given a glimpse of heaven have told this same truth. In all of your living, have you stored up anything in heaven, and has God released some of what you have stored up to remove your earthly debts?

I believe I am special, but I do not consider myself above anyone else. I encourage you to trust God and to allow yourself to be humbled through His powerful love. When I pulled up stakes in south Florida in January 2003 and moved to my father's house, I intended to stay there for no more than three months, but God had other notions about what I should do and about where I should be doing it. My drive to and from my job took three hours and 182 miles. That was a lot of wear on my vehicle and a large gas expense. I thought I could do much better by shortening my travel time and my expenditure on gas, saving money to afford my own space. I was also thinking so much about my car upkeep and my loan payments that God gave me a vision of my vehicle. I saw it parked in a space in front of the house, and when I opened the door I found the inside was aglow. Every inch of the interior was full of God's glorious golden light.

When I purchased the car, I also bought an expensive warranty that should have been honored nationwide so that I didn't have to spend vast sums of money for service or repairs. I had issues with this vehicle, and finally a national recall was instituted after government pressure on the manufacturer. Still, I lost a lot of money in the deal for this car because I bought it just as I was leaving the Northeast. But God saw my losses as well as my need for transportation.

The vehicle had an oil sludge problem due to design flaws, and this caused transmission and engine problems that were expensive to fix. When I filed for bankruptcy I was supposed to return the car to the company, but I did not. The company tried to repossess it but could not until seven years later. God spoke to me one night and said, "Get up and go get a new vehicle. Go to GM." I went with my wife the next day and was approved for a new vehicle. I then called the company that had been trying to repossess my first vehicle and said, "Be here at my address at 1 p.m. tomorrow and I will turn over the vehicle to you." The company took the car and sold it for about four thousand dollars, but God had ensured that I got full value for all of the repair costs I had shouldered on that vehicle before handing it over.

The Big Showdown

In October 2008 I was admitted to the hospital after my wife drove me to the emergency room. I had been there so many times that I had a history on file, allowing the triage process to proceed quite rapidly. Scans were ordered immediately since I was experiencing massive stomach pain, incessant vomiting, and overall sickness. CAT scans showed that my small intestines were tied up in a knot and that my bowel was out of line. I was taken to the intensive care unit right after doctors got the scan report, and my wife called our pastor, who came to the hospital. Other phone calls were made to prayer warriors, and so the doors of heaven were bombarded on my behalf. My pastor believed in laying on hands, and she did just that while praying for me.

My nephrologist, my primary doctor, and my surgeon, who was also the director of the hospital's surgical department, were all notified of my condition. The next morning another set of scans were done, and behold, my intestines had been unknotted and my bowel was in alignment again. In the evening my surgeon told us that further review showed my gallbladder was in distress and would probably have to come out, but he ordered more sophisticated scans that required medicine and dye to coat the organ for maximum clarity before the tests. The word went out to pray for my gallbladder, and my pastor laid hands on me before the coating began and the scans were taken. My surgeon returned the next day to say that there would be no surgery because the gallbladder had healed itself.

So what bad news or challenging condition would come next? Well, an EKG and a sonogram had been ordered as well, and the results showed that my heart was surrounded with water and that my liver did not look good at all. My blood pressure was raging in the 200-over-130 range. So the questions kept coming about my history regarding my liver and my heart and about my family history. Doctors told me I was in danger of a heart attack or a stroke, so I was put on a nitroglycerin drip and hooked up to a bevy of machines as I lay in the ICU. This happened early in the afternoon of my third day in the hospital. By early evening, there was a full-scale prayer service in the ICU, with two pastors, one evangelist, my wife, who was a deaconess, and my general surgeon, who was also a Christian believer. Later that evening, a church service was held for me. By morning when the newest set of scans was taken, everything was clear.

By late morning I was told that I could take liquids by mouth and that if I could keep them down, I would get a solid lunch and dinner. I was able to keep everything down, and by midnight the nitroglycerin drip and the other fluids I was getting were discontinued. Machines were disconnected with a note to the staff that if I could keep my breakfast down in the morning and if my blood pressure was in check, I would be discharged. My primary doctor came in the morning and saw that my blood pressure had been under control throughout the night and that I had kept my breakfast. "Nathan, we did absolutely nothing for you," he said. "It was all a divine intervention. I will do your discharge papers. Call my office to set up an appointment for a two-week follow-up."

Isn't God great? If He did this for me, He can do the same for you! I said I would discuss why the Devil could not conquer me, and the reason was simple. I was praying, other people near and far were praying, and most of all, God had a plan for me to fulfill on this earth. It is wise to surround yourself with strong prayer intercessors at all times. And you must pray for others when you pray for yourself. We were all entrusted with this responsibility by Jesus Christ in the Great Commission and even before He issued that directive.

When we pray to our Father, we say, "Forgive us our debts, as we also have forgiven our debtors" (Matthew 6:12). Some translations use the word *trespasses* instead of the word *debt*, but the meaning is the same. This passage is not about financial debt but about whatever is owed to someone in terms of repentance for wrongdoing. Prayer and forgiveness work together, because you must remove the plank from your own eye before you criticize someone else for the tiny speck in his eye or ask God to shower you with blessings. Jesus came to save the world's sick inhabitants, not those who are well and without stain of sin. Therefore, you must first place yourself in a position where you can be healed by Him.

When God gives you a task to do and you encounter difficulty whether with your health, your family, your job, or your church, you shouldn't throw up your hands and walk away or cuss someone out and quit. You must work through all of your difficulty until God releases you or you have completed the task.

When I lost my kidneys, my church was about to kick off its building program. I accomplished much from my hospital room. At home after release from the hospital, I used my telephone, my fax machine, and my computer to get things done. Contractor and subcontractor billings had to be proofed, approved, and submitted to the bank with proper documentation. Check drafts had to be submitted, checks reviewed and approved, payments made, and balances rectified. I had to keep up with many other church duties. I did not slack off, and God did not relax in protecting me. The Devil kept trying to deter and to defeat me, but God would not allow that! He will cover you just as He has covered me.

When I was hospitalized in October of 2008, the Devil attempted to render me unfit to receive the kidney transplant that was just around the corner. When you are on the transplant list, you must maintain a certain level of fitness to withstand the rigors of the transplant operation. If you are sick and risk rejecting a good kidney, you will be bypassed and the kidney will go to the next suitable person on the list. God did not want that to happen, and that is why He defeated the Devil. My kidney arrived in December 2008, and I was well enough to receive it. The night I received the kidney, my body temperature plummeted dramatically and I was in shock, so doctors had to work on me vigorously with heat treatments to revive my temperature and to alleviate the shock. I came out victorious after a long stay in the recovery room.

The kidney worked wonderfully and I no longer needed dialysis, but six months later, I felt that something was not right. I began to experience pain in the area of my new kidney. I called my nephrologist, and he told me to go straight to the hospital where he would fax an order for stat analysis and reports. The results indicated that I was in the first stages of a rejection. I had to go straight away to Orlando, Florida, to the transplant unit and to be admitted immediately. I was experiencing an antibody rejection and a cellular rejection, so a radical means of treatment began with Solu-Medrol and prednisone, using a plasma exchange method. Pieces of my kidney had to be pinched off for analysis without anesthesia, and the whole exercise was quite painful. The first day that I had the plasmapheresis procedure done on me, I went into anaphylaxis (a state of shock), and I was so cold that even though nurses put blankets on me, I kept asking for more to try to stop shaking and to feel some warmth.

On that first day of treatment, I did not eat but slept for about ten hours. The treatment had begun about nine-thirty in the morning, and at about nine in the evening I was awakened by a nurse who had been there in the morning at the end of her shift, had gone home for the day, and had just returned for her night shift. She knew I had not eaten all day, because the food tray was untouched. She told me she would get a fresh sandwich from the kitchen and asked what I wanted. The nurse insisted that I eat, because I needed to regain my strength. She had been there earlier and had seen how I was affected by this radical treatment. I got a sandwich, a fruit cup, some cookies, and a cup of hot tea. The remainder of the treatments went more smoothly since my body had become adjusted to the regimen.

Thirteen days passed before I was released from the hospital. Afterward, I visited the outpatient transplant clinic three times a week for a month, and then two times, and then once a week for six months before I was released back to my local nephrologist. Before I left the hospital, a woman came in and asked me if I was a pastor. I explained that I was a head deacon and not a pastor. She was a nursing tech who had visited me when I was not doing too well, and she had experienced something supernatural in the room. She told me she was a Christian, and even though she was not assigned to me that day, she wanted to speak to me. She had wondered who I was because she felt God's presence when she passed my room. I was in a private room in the ICU just across from the nursing station. We talked for a while, and she prayed God's continued blessings on me and left.

I had asked God why He allowed me to endure so much suffering, including the loss of my kidneys, and He had said, "So that you may have a testimony in your mouth, but know that I am your God and that I will heal you." Well, He is a promise keeper and I am living testimony that He is true to His word.

A few months before my kidney transplant our church had been built, and the dedication and grand opening took place. The church was beautiful and the Spirit of God evident. But within a few years the atmosphere was changing drastically as pride took root. When we build something with the help of God, we must keep Him in it to sanctify it continually, and we must keep ourselves grounded so that we don't attempt to rise above God Himself. When people have contributed and worked hard to build something, they want to be treated as though they are relevant even after the construction is over. God will speak to the head of an organization, but that does not preclude Him from speaking to others in the organization. Do we who are leaders listen to God only when we need to build but not after these structures are completed?

The Spirit of God began to show me one thing after another and requested my intervention in the situation, but I was rebuffed with disdain. The church began to come apart with members leaving, and the church was unable to pay its bills. The Spirit of God told me it was time to leave, but I had to wait for my wife. I had met her there, so it was hard for her to exit, but God promised me that He would show her a sign that it was time to leave. Before we left, I was ordained as an elder, but soon after the time came to go. My wife was accosted by the Spirit of God to see and to hear for herself the work of a wonton spirit that was certainly not His. She quickly realized that it was time to leave. We resigned and left immediately.

The Spirit of God continued to direct me and other people within my spiritual circle, encouraging me with His Word and with His promise, and by mid-2012, I had established a ministry that the Lord God had instructed me to create. We began worship in my home, and a year later, we rented a commercial space where we now worship. From the outside it does not look like much, but on the inside the Holy Spirit of God dwells. This is not a space I chose but the space that God chose for us. In 2013 I was ordained there as pastor with my friend from the Northeast, who is now a bishop, as the officiating and ordaining head.

In 2014 I was moved by the Spirit of God to contact my boyhood friend Shing, and I did so via Facebook. He had been living in another part of the United States with his family and was a devout Christian. We caught up on old times and on current events, but that was not the reason the Spirit of the Lord asked me to contact him. He was to perform a work ordained by God in the life of someone we both knew, and I was to make the connections. First he visited with me and my family in Florida and attended a Sunday service at our church. God allowed me to see the plans He had for him in his calling and had me prophesy to him that he too would be a pastor. Shing and I had talked about a potential appointment to deacon in his church a few months before he visited, and I was able to tell him that he would be the choice to fill that slot. He was God's choice, and he was appointed deacon by the board of directors.

January 2015 arrived and the younger brother of my first wife was very ill. After a hip replacement he contracted an infection that went unnoticed. Everyone thought he was alone and had no one close by to help him or to act as a liaison to his family hundreds of miles away, but God reminded me that Shing lived in his state, and I contacted my friend. I began to explain the situation to Shing, and he said, "I will go see him and find out what I can," before I told him where the young man lived and at what hospital he was being treated.

God directed him to say, "I will go forward to perform the Lord's will." This sick young man, who was now on his deathbed, had been refusing to come to Jesus. People had prayed for him many times and he had been asked, but he always replied, "I am not ready yet." But the Lord sent Shing to minister to him and to prepare his heart to finally say yes to God and to His Son. Shing also helped family members get face time with the young man on his cell phone just in case they did not make it to his bedside before he died. When they arrived. Shing was there to help them cope while they said their good-byes to their loved one. The young man's spirit went back to the arms of God. He accepted Jesus Christ, and the family was thankful and relieved in a time of grieving.

In late 2014, I was sitting in my living room, and after taking a break from reading the Scriptures I began to see a vision of God's golden light. Within that light rain came down from heaven in a constant downpour. God was showing me that He had not left me. My riches in glory were still flowing. I had been asking questions about the present and the future, because it seemed as though the persistent hammering of the Devil had isolated the ministry, keeping God's people from receiving His grace and His glory. God made it clear through His prophets that He has chosen the right people and will send them at the appointed time. God's timing is not the same as ours, so we must ignore the Devil's attempts and keep standing on God's Word. Before this He had shown me another vision of myself preaching and evangelizing to His people, who were unmoved by His Spirit. He has already selected those who will come to serve Him in spirit and in truth.

December of 2014 was an important month for me. On a visit to my nephrologist, I learned that my white blood-cell count was dangerously low. I had just recovered from a prolonged cold and a sinus infection and had been on antibiotics and steroids. My blood test results indicated that I was in danger of dying if I contracted another infection. The doctor immediately contacted a blood specialist in the medical group and asked that I make an appointment as soon as possible. The intended doctor was booked up for two months, and so I made an appointment with his partner. Since I had to go as soon as possible, I accepted an appointment for December 24, Christmas Eve.

God had communicated to me on three occasions through inanimate objects. A wooden sign had said, "God Is Love," and then an answering machine recording had said, "This message to pray is from the Spirit." Before going for my appointment, I had been praying to God about the visit and about the doctor I was going to see. I told God that since I had suffered so much pain, I did not want to endure any more during this visit. I knew that the usual recommendation was a spinal tap and an analysis. I told God that I did not want a spinal tap and that I needed a doctor who was knowledgeable and receptive to His direction.

A low white-cell count can also be a sign that cancer is present or imminent. When I was on dialysis I had a prolonged low white-cell count and was evaluated by blood specialists for cancer, but the tests came back negative. Medicines have side effects despite their abilities to help to heal, and some people develop cancer from using some of the stuff I take, but thank God I am free of cancer.

I showed up for my appointment, went through the check-in, and was taken to an examining room to await the doctor. I had never met the doctor or seen the doctor's picture. In the room I saw family pictures, but based on the doctor's first name, I still did not know whether this person was male or female. In a corner across from the family pictures, I saw religious items, little pillows and trinkets, and a cross. On a wall were three framed Scripture passages. The middle one was from the prophet Isaiah, and as I beheld it the glory of God came down on me and I began to weep. This is what God told me regarding my prayer: "So do not fear, for I am with you; do not be dismayed, for I am your God. I will strengthen you and help you; I will uphold you with my righteous right hand" (Isaiah 41:10).

The doctor came in a few minutes later. She was a woman and a Christian. She apologized for the delay and asked how I was doing. She said she had thought she was getting an easy case, but after reviewing my file she saw that I would pose a challenge. When she asked how I was doing, I said I was tired because I had not slept much in the last few days. She looked up from her papers, and I explained that I was a pastor and had been under attack spiritually and had been awakened to pray. I said I was sometimes up for hours before I could go back to sleep. She told me that God sometimes awakened her during the night to pray and to speak with her. We discussed being Christians and doing the work of God, and she said, "Mr. Palus, you are going to make me cry." I told her, "I saw your Scripture verses here on the wall, and while I was waiting I was in tears, because God was speaking to me through Isaiah 41:10." I told her how I had prayed to God to place me in the right place and in the right hands and said He had now assured me that I was in the right place and that she was the right person.

I had to take a blood test before leaving the facility. I was scheduled for my next visit and a blood test that morning. Returning for my next visit, I learned that the results of the blood test taken on the first visit had come back normal, with no sign of a low white blood-cell count. The results of the second test came back normal, and third test also showed no indication of low white-blood cell count. God did a miracle in my life. When I showed up for my third visit with the blood specialist, she immediately said, "Mr. Palus, I see only sick people. You don't have to come back anymore." She said I didn't have to make another appointment, but if a problem arose, I could come in and she would see me.

I know God did a miracle in my life, but my nephrologist had also done something the last time I was in his office. He had adjusted the dosage of one of my immune suppressant drugs. That helped but I will never mistake the work of man for the work of God! Sometimes the Enemy uses natural occurrences in our lives to hide the supernatural and to deter us from giving the glory to God. When I went and saw my doctor again and he pointed out that he had reduced my medication, I acknowledged that and did not try to minimize the effect of his actions, because God's mighty hands had guided him while he treated me.

This concludes my testimony, and although I could not testify that I had been strung out on drugs or had been in jail for twenty years before God saved me, I hope my story is no less relevant to hurting souls. Don't say that you are waiting until you get your life together before you come to God, because we can never be perfect, and we need God to help us.

Let us pray right now. Almighty God, I accept Jesus Christ Your Son as my Lord and my Savior. I confess that I am a sinner and ask for Your forgiveness. I repent of my sins, and I ask for Your cleansing by the shed blood of Jesus Christ right now in His name! Lord, cover me right now with Your Holy Spirit and fill the voids in my life.

In closing, I ask you to read these Scripture passages: Isaiah 43:2, 1 Corinthians 3:18–21, and James 1:5–6.

May God bless you all.

Notes

"Children of One God"
Genesis 2
Proverbs 1:7
Romans 3:23
John 1:1
2 Timothy 2:15–16
2 Timothy 2:17
2 Timothy 2:19
Isaiah 55:6–7
Isaiah 65:1
Isaiah 65:2
John 3:16

"New Year's Resolutions vs. Resolutions of Faith"
Hebrews 11:1
Exodus 3:4
Exodus 3:5
Exodus 3:5–10
Exodus 3:11
Exodus 2:14
2 Timothy 1:7

"The 'What If' Question"
Proverbs 10:8
1 Corinthians 13:11
Acts 9:1–12
Acts 9:17
Acts 9:18–19
Genesis 2:7
Genesis 1:26
Genesis 1:2
Job 26:13
Psalm 33:6
John 20:21–22

"Oh, the Chatter!"
2 Corinthians 12:10
John 10:10

"Who Is the Thief?"
John 8:34
John 8:43–44

"Thievery Will Attempt Your Overthrow"
Exodus 4:18–19
Exodus 4:20
Exodus 3 :13–15
Exodus 4:21–23
Proverbs 1:7
Genesis 17:9–14
Exodus 4:24–26
Genesis 1:1
Exodus 4:14
Exodus 4:25

"Temptation Is Sin's Call to Human Nature"
Genesis 3:7
Genesis 3:6
Psalm 119:105
Matthew 3, 4
Matthew 3:16–17
Matthew 21
Mark 11
Matthew 4:3
Matthew 4:4
Genesis 3:1–5
Fannie J. Crosby, "Rescue the Perishing"

"Generational Things"
Romans 1:18–19
Romans 1:21
Romans 1:28–32

"When Good Intentions Come with a But"
Daniel Keyes, *Flowers for Algernon*
John 3:16
Revelation 3:20
Ephesians 3:20–21

"We Struggle with Ill-Conceived Plans"
Ecclesiastes 1:9
1 Chronicles 14:10
1 Chronicles 14:14–15
1 Chronicles 14:16–17
Proverbs 29:18
Hosea 4:6

"Acting without God"
1 Chronicles 13

1 Samuel 5, 6
1 Samuel 6:20
1 Chronicles 13:12
1 Chronicles 15
Job 12:15–16
Ecclesiastes 9:11

"New in America"
Jeremiah 17:9

"Graduating into Adulthood"
Romans 8:28

"Searching for the Elusive Ladder"
Genesis 39

"Climbing the Ladder of Hope Again"
Luke 16:19

"The Big Showdown"
Matthew 6:12
Isaiah 41:10
Isaiah 43:2
1 Chronicles 3:18–21
James 1:5–6

Resources

Armstrong, W. P. *Ancient Figs of the Holy Land*, vol. 5, no.1 (Spring 1996); accessed February 7, 2015; http://waynesword.Palomar.edu/vernal2c.htm.

Moffett, James, and McElheny, Kenneth R., eds. *Points of View: An Anthology of Short Stories.* Mentor, 1966

Keyes, Daniel. *Flowers for Algernon.* New York: Harcourt, Brace & World, 1966.

Robertson, Ian. *Society: A Brief Introduction.* New York: Worth Publishers, Inc., 1989.

Printed in the United States
By Bookmasters